BALTIC COUNTDOWN

BALTIC COUNTDOWN

A NATION VANISHES

Peggie Benton

OPEN ROAD

INTEGRATED MEDIA
NEW YORK

ISBN: 978-1-5040-8869-5

This edition published in 2023 by Open Road Integrated Media, Inc.
180 Maiden Lane
New York, NY 10038
www.openroadmedia.com

Latvia, as one of the Baltic States, existed for only twenty years. At the end of this book there is a brief account of the country's historical background.

For those who suffered and did not survive

INTRODUCTION

One of the saddest of the forgotten tragedies of our times was the destruction of the Baltic States. The peoples of Estonia, Latvia and Lithuania had long and very complex histories behind them when they were brought under Russian rule in the course of the 18th century. (Lithuania had once been the strongest power in Eastern Europe.) But with the revolution in Russia and the defeat of Germany in 1918 they managed to break free, fighting off the Bolsheviks and proclaiming their independence.

It was to last for just twenty years. In 1939 the fate of these small lands was decided by Hitler and Stalin as part of the deal which set off the attack on Poland and started the Second World War. In the summer of 1940 the Russians moved in, pretending that they had been invited. Behind the Red Army came the scavengers, for the NKVD (as the old CHEKA, now the KGB, was then called) followed up the Soviet army as the Gestapo followed up the Reichswehr; and the Communist party secretaries followed the NKVD as the Gauleiters followed the Gestapo. In no time at all the Baltic lands were Sovietized and Russianized, their living standards brought down, their free institutions abolished, the fabric of their lives in ruins. As far as is known some 170,000 of the best, most active and enterprising citizens were rounded up, arrested and sent off to Siberia.

It was not until much later that the full extent of this vile operation was understood. It had been planned long in advance, its details laid down with bleak precision in the notorious Order No. 001223, signed in October 1939 by Beria's right-hand man, Ivan Serov. Nobody knew much about this story at the time. The Russians struck, characteristically, when the attention of the world was focused on the desperate battle for Paris. After the fall of France our minds were on other things; and later still the revelation of Nazi wickedness on an almost unimaginable scale, coupled with our desire to give our new allies the benefit of the doubt, stood between us and the Russian reality. Post-war bullying and brutality, most blatantly in Hungary and Czechoslovakia, have made it easier for people to credit Russian atrocities, such as the massacre in the Katyn Forest. But still all too little is known about the tragedy of the Baltic States, now treated as a constituent part of the Soviet Union and heavily settled by Russians.

That is why I so welcome Mrs Benton's book. She was there, in Riga, when the Russians came—and during all the time their coming was being prepared. She knew about foreign occupations because she had lived through the Nazi invasion of Austria—an invasion none the less real even though many countries welcomed it and worked for it: many did not. She had been in the Baltic region long enough to learn a good deal about the people and their history. She could identify herself with their hopes without idealizing them. And she could appreciate the cultural shock, as well as the human tragedy, of an occupation that soon became an outright annexation, and an annexation which entailed a revolution, but a revolution conducted by foreigners with guns. She writes simply and without pretence from her own experience and from what she learnt from her

Baltic friends, as well as from her official work as an analyst of the Russian press. She brings home to the reader very vividly indeed, it seems to me, what it is like to be in a small country whose quiet ways, offensive to none, are wantonly trampled out of existence by a bully without scruple. There is a good deal to be learnt from her book, not only about the Baltic States in general and Latvia in particular, to which it is a memorial, but also about how people are likely to behave when confronted with a power which seems too strong to fight but which cannot be appeased.

It is not, however, a solemn book. It is full of diverting incident, not least the journey home—an escape really, all across Russia to Vladivostok, through the only gap in the German encirclement.

Edward Crankshaw

BALTIC COUNTDOWN

CHAPTER 1

Raindrops, sluggish with cold, slid down the outer panes of the double windows in the gathering dusk. From the high ceiling an unshaded bulb glared harshly on the faded group of armchairs, and the wooden partition which divided room No. 22 of the Hotel St Petersburg, Riga, and hid the massive Russian bed from the sight of visitors. Beside this stood a couple of suitcases—all that we were sure of possessing in the world.

It was October 12th, 1938. Two months before, my husband's chief, Tommy Kendrick, head of the Passport Control Office in Vienna, had been expelled from Austria on a charge of espionage, and when the Gestapo began to arrest his 'accomplices' we had been told by the Foreign Office to leave for Riga within twenty-four hours.

But this was not so easy. Six months earlier, the Germans had without warning occupied Austria and now they were threatening Czechoslovakia. Our route to Riga lay through Prague, Warsaw and Kaunas, the capital of Lithuania. Already the land frontiers of Czechoslovakia were closed and most of the staff of our Prague Legation evacuated to London. Hungarian and Polish troops were mobilizing in order to snatch disputed strips of territory from their stricken neighbour. Trains to Prague were at a standstill and planes already over-booked. However, with the help of our Dutch colleagues we managed the two hops to Warsaw by KLM, and next day, the final stages of the journey, the aeroplanes becoming smaller and the days shorter as we progressed northwards.

On our arrival in Riga, Kenneth went off to report for duty and I sat alone, bereft at one stroke of the home we had set up six months earlier (now impounded and sealed by the Gestapo), our friends, an interesting job and even, for the moment, of anything to read or do.

A thermometer was fixed between the two windows and as I gazed at the congealing raindrops its crimson thread sank slowly towards freezing point.

Only five years before, I had left Riga, resolved never to return.

CHAPTER 2

Next morning a watery sun gleamed on the puddles in the Castle Square. Kenneth set out for the Consulate. He had returned quite cheerful the evening before.

'The building's a bit old-fashioned. It faces a park which runs along the Canal. The Consular offices are in the front—quite imposing and must be pleasant in summer. The Passport Control Office is in the servants' quarters and I should think our main office must have been the kitchen. There's the usual counter and a row of hard chairs for the visa applicants, but the lino stops short at our door, as well as the trimmings. The rest of our work goes on in a series of rooms leading from a long dark passage. One of them may have been the larder, or else the architect got his sums wrong and had a little bit of space left over, not that it matters, since no one works there.'

'And what about the staff?'

'The Consul, Henry Hobson, is a bluff sort of chap and seems to know what he's doing. The senior Vice-Consul, Glyn Hall, has lived here for years and is thoroughly dug in. Apart from that there are a couple of girls married to Latvians, a locally employed Vice-Consul and the usual solid, respectable Consular Messengers complete with basic English.'

'And the P.C.O.?'

'As you know, Nick in is charge. Ex-Black Watch with no family and no obvious cares, and the most incredibly polished shoes. Then there is Dorothy Corrie from one of the Anglo-Baltic families. She speaks fluent Russian, has lots of local knowledge and an unshakably British outlook.'

'Anyone else?'

'Just Paul. His father and mother have lived here since the Baltic States gained their independence from Russia after the '14–'18 war. When the family fled from Moscow at the time of the Revolution, poor Paul was somehow left behind with his nurse and it was months before they were picked up by some refugee organization and reunited with his parents. I don't think he has ever quite got over it. Don't underestimate him, though. He speaks the three local languages fluently and he has a photographic memory.'

The days at the Hotel St Petersburg, or *Peterpils Viesnica,* to use the Latvian name painted over the door, passed slowly. There was no news of our luggage and, without a typewriter or wireless set, we had no home diversions but a writing pad, a pack of patience cards and a few books we had been able to borrow. It was no use looking for a flat until our furniture arrived, so we decided to move into the apartment of Madame Mossolova, widow of a White Russian general, who took in odd foreigners and 'language officers'. Since the Soviet Union was closed to visits by members of our Armed Forces, British officers studying for a Russian interpretership were distributed between Riga, Tallinn (the capital of Estonia) and Helsinki. To learn in one year what their American counterparts were only expected to master in two, meant steady application, and as the young men were boarded out in respectable households they were denied the convenience of a 'sleeping dictionary'.

The flat in the Elizabetes iela, halfway between the Legation and the Consulate, was rambling, dark and filled with heavy drapes and furniture from Tsarist times. Olga Mossolova, a thin authoritative woman with the enduring quality of whipcord, chatted across the long table during meals, in Russian or French or slightly hesitant English, according to the nationality of the guest she was addressing. Between courses she drew impatiently at the long cardboard mouthpiece of her *papirossi,* discarding one after another until the crystal ash tray was overflowing. For every meal the table was laid with a starched damask cloth, cut glass and heavy Russian silver.

'It is a pleasure to use such beautiful things, Madame,' I said to her after we had been there a few days.

'Ah this,' she replied in her deep voice, 'is nothing. My husband was governor of a province. We had a staff of seventeen indoor servants and a dozen house guests at a time. But, do you know, I never went inside the kitchen. I was not even sure where it was. You see, I was only a child when we married and my husband took care of everything. Now, I think I have become quite a good housekeeper. You will never find bought vodka in my home.'

She pointed to three cut-glass decanters filled with yellow, gold and pale green liquid. A careful *ménagère,* madame told us, would never buy ready-made vodka but go to a chemist's and get a bottle of pure alcohol. This was then warmed in a saucepan and the fusel oil burnt off with a lighted match. A measured quantity of distilled water was added and the whole brew flavoured with lemon or orange peel, or the Polish *zubravka* grass which gave a subtle flavour and a delicate green hue.

'I offer small glasses, but in the old days . . .' Her eyes glowed with memories of the expansive life of Imperial Russia.

She turned abruptly to Dorothy Corrie, who lived permanently in the flat. 'Noble has passed his exam. I had a letter from him today.'

'And what about Thurloe?'

'Failed. And he with a Russian wife. I think she wanted too much to learn English.' She crushed another *papirossa* into the ash tray. 'And who will have a bath tonight?'

It was the custom in the older blocks of Riga flats to provide the tenants with hot water from a central boiler once a week. Early in the morning the maids would start to wash the household linen, which was then hung in the basement to dry. Although a bath was available at any time, provided one had the patience to wait while the wood in the tall copper stove burnt through, Madame Mossolova naturally encouraged her guests to take advantage of the free hot water on washing day.

We had always been impressed by the luxurious Hollywood image of a sunken bath. Here, for the first time, we were to enjoy one. The bathroom was large and drably tiled. The taps were of massive brass and the W.C. bore the name DREADNOUGHT, trade mark of an English manufacturer and a relic of the supremacy of the *sanitation anglaise*. The huge enamelled bath, perhaps owing to some misunderstanding on the part of the builder, was sunk right into the floor, its varicosed rim flush with the encaustic tiles. It was not until one lay in the steaming water and gazed upwards that the problem of accommodating the bath's volume was explained. From the ceiling hung the naked cast-iron belly of the bath in the flat above, its runaway pipe snaking exposed down the wall. Lying in the bath one was enjoying space normally belonging to one's neighbour below, whilst inside the bulge above one's head the occupant of the flat above might even now be lying naked.

Every morning after breakfast Kenneth walked to the office

and I went back to our bedroom overlooking the blank brick wall of a narrow courtyard. Cars from a garage below tainted the air with the curious fumes of the local petrol, which was mixed with thirty per cent of the potato spirit used to make Latvian vodka.

On fine days I would walk through the gardens on the banks of the canal which divided the original Hanseatic town from the nineteenth century city. The old town had been encircled by walls which were demolished in 1857, and the canal was the moat which once protected them. Originally, the houses of the Baltic German settlers were confined within these walls. The tall dwellings of the merchants, housing floor upon floor of store-rooms beneath tiled and gabled roofs, jostled patrician mansions with their stone portals and chevron-built shutters. Here and there, in a courtyard, a tree reached for the sun.

On the river front below the castle, carts loaded with goods for shipment rattled over the cobbles behind horses with high wooden yokes over their necks. A small steam ferry plied between the castle and the industrial suburbs of Kipsala and Ilgeciems. Upriver, the road was carried over the Daugava by a pontoon bridge half a kilometre long, with the girder arches of the railway bridge rising beyond it.

One day I followed the river downstream to the Export Harbour, where ships were loading with timber, hemp and dairy products, and bundles of king veitch, exported to Scotland for colouring whisky, now that the sherry casks from Spain were becoming so expensive. This quay held a special memory for me.

Five years earlier I, with my small sons, had been asked to spend the summer on the estate of Baron Kruedener, the father of the man I was to marry. We arrived by sea in a small German coaster from Stettin. As we sailed up the Daugava to Riga three great churches dominated the skyline—St Peter's with the tallest wooden spire in Europe, built tier upon tier; the *Dom,* its galleried tower swelling with the graceful lines of a Georgian silver teapot and St James's spire, slender and hexagonal. All of them copper-sheathed, gleamed in the evening light. The air was warm and Jimmy, my future husband, was waiting on the quay.

Even in early May it was still light when, after leaving the train at the country station of Tukums and driving for four hours through deep forest and rolling fields, we reached Rindseln. Life was exciting—a new door opening. The lovely summer days passed quickly, but beneath the surface lay financial worries. It seemed that Jimmy's best hope of employment lay in Germany, where the Nazis were becoming increasingly aggressive, while the economic situation was depressing wages. There seemed no prospect of ever being able to send the boys to school in England. For all the Baron's ingenious schemes and his wife's thrift, Rindseln was bringing in barely enough to cover expenses.

'You know,' Kruedener confided to me one day, 'cards are my only source of ready cash. When I'm in Riga I play every evening at the Musse, the club where we Balts have been winning—and losing—money for the last two hundred years. It's not that my bridge is so good. It's just that I can stay awake longer than anyone else.'

The situation was precarious and my brother, a medical student, was so concerned that he thumbed a passage in a Lithuanian freighter and came to Rindseln to persuade me to return. In those days there would have been no haven in England if Jimmy were without a job or our marriage went wrong. There was no Welfare State and no Health Service to ensure survival. My mother, for all her loyalty and initiative, could do little to help since her pension, as a general's widow, was only £150 a year. As long as the boys were dependent, my alimony was a precious hedge against destitution.

So, with great sadness, Jimmy and I agreed to part. A door had closed, I thought for ever.

Now, it was as if a great pendulum had swung, reversing the past. I was beginning life in Latvia once more. This time our situation was secure, but winter loomed ahead like a long, dark tunnel.

As my future home, Latvia and its history had interested me deeply, but I had absorbed, inevitably, the Baltic German point of view, which regarded the country from the standpoint of a colonizing power. Yet the Latvians had developed an indigenous culture and were trading fine weapons and ornaments forged of gold, silver and bronze with places as far afield as Rome, Baghdad, Basra and Isfahan when both we and the Germans were not yet civilized.

Latvia's natural wealth, added to excellent harbours, which were starting points for trade routes to Russia and the East, made it a tempting prey for Vikings, Danes, Hanseatic traders, the warlike knights of the Teutonic and Livonian Orders and, in their turn, the Poles. Even England was involved in the competition and in 1558 sent arms to Ivan the Terrible, who made use of them in a scorched earth campaign against Erik XIV of Sweden in the course of which he put the northern half of the country to the torch and the sword. Most of the towns were levelled and 'over great stretches of the land no human voice could be heard, nor even the barking of a dog'.

The Cross accompanied the sword, and missionaries of the Greek Orthodox Church clashed with Catholics, while the southern half of the country was for centuries involved in the struggle between the Protestant states headed by Sweden and the Catholic group led by Poland.

Until the independence of Latvia was proclaimed on November 18th, 1918, the country was divided into three sections, often ruled by different foreign powers—Livonia in the north, Courland to the south, and Latgale, marching with the Russian border. Under a succession of semi-independent dukes, Courland achieved a degree of prosperity. Duke James, 'too rich for a duke and too poor for a king', as Charles XI of Sweden described him, supplied our Charles I with six men-of-war built of Courland oak and complete with cannon, muskets and provisions. When the King failed to pay the bill the Duke hedged his bet by signing a treaty of non-aggression with Cromwell. This was used as a pretext by Charles II for offering him in payment only a small island at the mouth of the Gambia River, which was good for nothing but a little pearl fishing.

Peter the Great, seeking an outlet to the Baltic, drove the Swedes out of Livonia and took over the independent city of Riga. The Baltic barons were quick to realize the advantages of co-operation with Russia, and though a centralized system of administration was imposed, most of the governors of the new provinces were Balts who, with their administrative ability, soon occupied nearly half the important positions in the Russian Government and Armed Forces.

In 1817 the serfs of the Baltic Provinces were freed, but at the same time the land they had acquired was sequestered in compensation, it was declared, for the loss of their labour. The serfs were free as birds—but free to starve. In spite of this, and the introduction of a government poll tax and compulsory military service the peasants, probably as a reaction against former domination by the Balts, pinned their hopes on the Russians.

Following the 'russification' campaign of Alexander III, corrupt and inefficient bureaucrats swarmed into the country. Freedom of the press was abolished, the powers of the secret police were extended to cover the area and denunciations and deportations became common. Wholesale conversions to the Orthodox faith were achieved by means of bribery and Russian became the official language.

Riga, however, was becoming the most advanced city in Russia. A Latvian middle class was established and peasants left their homes and settled in the cities to form a growing industrial proletariat, though Balts still held the most important positions in industry, commerce, banking, education and medicine. In 1905 peasant uprisings against the Baltic landowners were ruthlessly suppressed, too late to prevent the looting and burning of scores of estates. The Latvian leader, Karl Ulmanis, was sent into exile.

With the coming of independence the position of middle-class Balts was little affected, but the landowners, their estates reduced to fifty hectares each, lost the power they had held so long and were obliged to eke out a modest existence in the country, or look for employment.

These landowners, though acknowledging their German origin, insisted on their status as Balts and, whilst regarding Latvian achievements with reluctant admiration, their attitude towards both the Russians and the Germans was tinged with contempt. The former they regarded as incompetent and often crude, and the latter as narrow-minded, conformist and somewhat provincial.

'There have been many outstanding Balts, including Madame de Stäel and her pen-friend, my ancestor Madame Kruedener,' the baron told me, adding with pleasant cynicism, 'but we *are* a bit inbred and if you go to any estate and look around you'll probably find the family idiot up a tree.'

This expectation had kept the boys interested during the visits we sometimes paid to neighbouring estates. There were signs of inbreeding, a certain defeatist lassitude amongst some of the Balts, but we saw nothing stranger than a squirrel in a tree top.

'My great-grandmother was a foundling who was brought to Riga during the cholera epidemic in Hamburg', Kruedener said one day. 'Goodness knows what kind of blood she brought into the family. Whatever it was, it was welcome. She was a survivor, like me.'

In spite of the loss of estates which before the war had covered over thirty thousand acres Kruedener displayed no resentment. The great house at Rindseln had been burned down and the family now lived in the low wooden building formerly used by the bailiff. But there was still excellent shooting, and riding through the firebreaks out in the forest, and plenty of food for the family. The mill and the forge and the great barn and dairies which had made the estate into a self-sufficient unit had been allotted each to a peasant proprietor.

'Quite irrational', commented Kruedener. 'Formerly all this was used by everyone. A peasant had his share of the produce and could bring his wood to the mill and his grain to be threshed. Now, the buildings are falling into disrepair. None of the peasants can keep sufficient animals to manure his fields or afford machinery to work his holding, though I must say that the State has made a good job of the big dairy co-operatives, and exports are booming—particularly to your country.

'The landowners were wrong to despise the Latvians,' he continued. 'They're tough and intelligent, wonderful craftsmen with a feeling for timber and natural materials, and whatever the stories put about by my people, they're clean to the point of destructiveness. It's not so difficult to keep things clean once they're in order, but after the devastation of the last war I've seen them polishing the few remaining panes of glass in a window or scrubbing a shell-torn floor. Of course, they're a bit surly, but after so many years as under-dogs, who wouldn't be?'

The Latvian passion for order was evident in Riga. In spite of the mixture of races and traditions, the town was run with doll's house neatness. Under the drifting clouds of autumn large yellow leaves floated down from the trees and formed jagged patterns on the glistening pavements. But they were not allowed to lie, and in the parks, women with clean kerchiefs over their heads moved about ceaselessly in pairs, carrying small wooden stretchers on to which they gathered the leaves as they fell and tidied them away.

The language problem was tackled just as methodically. The Latvian language, though of considerable philological interest, is of little use outside the frontiers, and there was no incentive for foreigners to learn more than the limited amount which concerned their daily needs.

But the Latvians, clinging to this symbol of their heritage, had a very high standard of literacy, even through the periods when the teaching of Latvian was suppressed or limited in the schools. So with Independence in 1918 there was a surge of interest in the vernacular. In order to purify the language of distortions a department of philology was opened in the State University. As new words are constantly needed to keep a language up to date, a small cash reward was offered to anyone inventing an acceptable Latvian equivalent for a modern foreign word. These new Latvian words were listed in the local newspapers.

Unless one were content to walk everywhere it was essential to know the Latvian names for the Post Office, the railway stations, the Central Market, and so on, otherwise bus or tram conductors would refuse to issue a ticket. Numbers were vital too, as stamps were sold on the same basis. German and Russian were current in the shops, but most of the business in the market was conducted in Latvian by the peasant women who sold fruit and berries and fresh vegetables in summer and, all the year round, delicious dairy products, fresh fish and game. It is surprising how quickly one learns the essential words when one is interested or hungry.

Winter was tightening its grip and drawing the sap deep into the earth. The wide clear skies of early autumn had shrunk to a grey blanket pressing down on the leafless branches and clustered roofs of the city.

The sense of claustrophobia was overwhelming. The two small states of Latvia and Estonia lay side by side between the mute boundaries of Russia and the sea. Below these two, Lithuania, with Poland on her east and East Prussia to the south, completed a trio bound, it seemed, to remain on the sidelines of international events.

But though space was confined, time could be extended, and I decided to explore backwards into the history of the country and to discover more of the Latvian point of view. Unfortunately, I could not read the Latvian language and owing to political prejudices accounts in other languages were hardly likely to be helpful. I needed some personal contact. The various racial groups established in the country tended to mix very little, and even the Anglo-Russian families, some established for four generations or more, limited most of their social contacts to their compatriots and some White Russians and Balts.

One day, however, when I was visiting the Consulate, a thin grey-haired man with wire-framed glasses approached me timidly. 'I am Pekšens, professor of history at the State University, and I like very much to learn English. I study, but I need conversation. Do you know where I can find it?'

I suggested that we might meet and talk from time to time. The Professor's vocabulary was extensive but the sentences flowed awkwardly, so when he was caught up in a subject he would lapse into German, the *lingua franca* of the Baltic States. This was fun for me, but bad value for him; however, he seemed quite happy about it.

It was only after several meetings with Pekšens that I learnt, to my surprise, that we were living under a dictatorship. One was so used to the stereotypes—black shirts, brown shirts, hoarse cries of '*Duce, Duce*' and 'Heil Hitler', thumping boots and sudden disappearances—that one accepted any country with a peaceful tenure of life and plenty of individual freedom as a democracy. And this *had* been Latvia's status when I left in 1933.

When Latvia gained independence the Government set to work in a mood of optimism. Democracy, which they had chosen, meant freedom, so anyone was free to form a political party, with the result that some of the parties in the *Saeima*, the Latvian parliament, had less than ten members. The outcome was confusion and compromise and, as usually happens in a troubled situation, corruption crept in, encouraged by economic depression. Constitutional reform was blocked by hard-headed parties of the Left and Right. The Communists were building strategically placed blocks of flats, potential fortresses like the Karl Marxhof in Vienna, and the Nazi 'Nationalists' were running a clandestine Hitler Youth Movement.

By early 1934 things had reached such a pitch that there was a real fear of civil war. In May, just as in Estonia two months earlier, the government declared a state of siege and the *Saeima* was dissolved. Some of the left wing deputies were arrested and later released, and the Communist Party went underground. A Government of National Unity was declared by President Ulmanis and General Balodis, both old fighters for Latvian independence, and since then things had gone along quietly,

Ulmanis having declared that he would only stay in office until constitutional reforms had been carried out. But that was four years ago.

Towards the end of November our belongings arrived, neatly packed beneath the Gestapo seals, and we moved into a flat in one of the old-fashioned apartment houses in the Ausekla iela, just opposite the dock where the ships left for the outside world. Someone had told us that Reginald Urch, for many years *Times* correspondent in Moscow and afterwards in Riga, was being transferred to Helsinki and no longer needed the maid who had been in his employ for seventeen years.

One chilly afternoon we called on Urch in the small wooden house where he was just packing up. 'Lotte is an original,' he said, 'a white witch one might say. At some phases of the moon she's strange, but she can cook, and if she takes a fancy to you, all her spells will be benign. Are you a good housekeeper?'

I hesitated. 'I like a comfortable home and good food, and a clean bathroom and kitchen . . .'

The interview was turning out a little differently from my expectations, as it seemed that it was I who was being put to the test. Lotte, having evidently decided to use Urch as her representative, was not at home.

'I think you'll suit each other. Lotte is not very fond of dusting ornaments, but when you can write your name on the top of your desk she'll understand, and for a week or two everything will be spotless. Lotte is honest and speaks good German,' said Urch as we parted. 'We are very fond of her. I hope you will thank me.'

When we arrived at the flat Lotte was waiting outside the tall varnished front door, a stout woman in her fifties, wearing a tight black coat. Her large floury face had the pallor of a freshly picked mushroom and her frizzy hair had obviously been tinted with henna, but not for some time. The gaps in her front teeth gave them an individuality which seemed to suggest that they, too, were involved in any conversation and her eyes, the red-brown of a faithful setter, appeared a little out of focus.

Two men in blue uniforms, each with a length of rope coiled round his waist, were standing beside her with our suitcases at their feet. Each wore a cap with a brass badge reading respectively FIX and FAX.

Without any formal greeting to us Lotte weighed in on the two freelance porters, who earned a living by wheeling bundles and boxes from one point in the city to another.

'Wipe your feet. Put the luggage down there.' She slapped into their outstretched hands half the amount we should have ventured to offer and closed the door firmly. We were evidently hired.

The front door opened straight into a large dining room. From this, one door led to a drawing room which in summer would look into the green tops of the plane trees in the street outside. Next to it was our bedroom. A long passage, dark and narrow, skirted an unprepossessing bathroom, Lotte's bedroom and the kitchen, and culminated in the guest room where the boys were to sleep during the holidays. This room, with its open view, gave one something of the relief experienced as a train comes out of a tunnel.

While Lotte bustled off to the shops we opened one packing case after another, pulling out books and treasures, savouring the joys of having a home once more. Nothing of value had been taken. Only some letters and diaries and a perfectly harmless parody of Fletcher's 'Hassan', written by our colleagues in Vienna about the clients in the Visa Office, were missing. We hoped that somewhere in Berlin the Gestapo were puzzling about the meaning of the verses.

CHAPTER 3

For Christmas 1938 we were given home leave, but first we had to take a Bag down to the Legation in Kaunas on our way to catch the boat in Memel. The United Baltic Corporation ran a line of cargo ships with some passenger accommodation, and we were to sail in the BALTEAKO, one of the smaller vessels. At this time of the year there would be no other passengers.

Kenneth had never acted as King's Messenger before but legends of spies in transcontinental expresses—and even our recent brush with the Gestapo—added a touch of excitement as we boarded the Berlin train.

'Don't let the Bag out of your sight,' said Hobson, the Consul. 'Take it into the dining car for meals. If one of you goes to the loo, the other must stay with it. The Berlin Express will be stuck full of Germans.'

Our first-class compartment was empty until the train, with a final clang from the engine bell, drew out of the station. Then a tall German, his face seamed with duelling scars, came down the corridor and, after peering into the carriages on either side, moved in with us. When we went to the restaurant car he followed us. As we finished our coffee, he too rose. At the Lithuanian frontier he presented only a thin leather brief case

20

to the Customs officials, who waived it away. Kenneth was, *ex officio*, immune from search, but my suitcase was lifted down from the rack, opened and riffled through with the bored, busy-body air that so many Customs men adopt.

Arrived at Kaunas, we piled our things into one of the waiting droshkies which rolled soundlessly over the cobbles on its elephantine rubber tyres.

In the constricting cold of early December the town looked infinitely drab, making one appreciate, in retrospect, the imposing streets of Riga. Kaunas was a makeshift capital, formerly a small garrison town, and patchily modernized after the loss of Vilnius to Poland during the frontier squabbles which followed the First War. Though a few tasteless modern buildings had been put up in the centre and some of the streets were paved, most of the houses were low-built to allow the defenders a clear field of fire—a precaution understandable in this case, since it was here that Napoleon crossed the Niemen on his march to Moscow.

Our room was booked at the Hotel Metropole, a name which led us to hope for a certain standard of comfort. But once more, I found myself sitting in a hotel bedroom of anachronistic drabness while Kenneth washed off the smoke of the train and set out for the Legation with the precious Bag.

It was some time before he returned. Tom Preston, the Chargé d'Affaires, felt isolated in Kaunas and was only too happy to chat with someone from the metropolis of Riga.

'And what about the Bag?' I asked. 'Everything all right?'

'I suppose so,' Kenneth replied a little flatly. 'As a matter of fact, Preston didn't even open it. He just said "Thank goodness my laundry's back from Riga. There's no one here who can iron a dress shirt properly". He asked if we were enjoying the Baltic States and said that one of his colleagues had described them as "solid, stolid and squalid". He obviously didn't know them very well.'

We had been warned that meals were served late at the Metropole, but after waiting till ten on the first evening we found the waiters still in their shirt sleeves when we went down to dinner. They may well have expected to spend the evening on their own, as there was only one other guest. This was a stocky man wearing his dark hair combed in inky strands across his bald head, and a well-preserved suit. He ate his dinner in abstracted concentration while the waiters fussed over him and scrambled for the loose change he left on the tablecloth. It was midnight before the black coffee which ended the meal was served, with slices of lemon and lumps of the hard sugar which is meant to be held between the teeth so that the hot liquid can be sucked through it.

Next day a message came from the Legation to say that our sailing would be delayed owing to engine trouble. Mr Preston would like Mr Benton to call round at eleven. We were to lunch with him at one, so I was intrigued to know what business might need attending to in the meantime.

'As a matter of fact, it was a musical morning,' said Kenneth surprisingly when he called to pick me up. 'Tom Preston is writing the score for a ballet. His wife, who is Russian, is in England at the moment and his daughter is a ballet dancer, so you see . . .'

During lunch Preston reminisced about the murder of the Tsar and his family at Ekaterinburg in the summer of 1918. He had been Consul at Tomsk at the time, quite near in Siberian terms.

'One thing I am sure of,' he said. 'It was the advance of the White Russians which put paid to the Imperial family. The Bolsheviks couldn't risk their being used as a rallying point, and what might have been their salvation actually sealed their doom. The Russians didn't announce their deaths until the end of December, 1925, and then perhaps only to discourage impostors. With so much Romanoff treasure still waiting abroad to be claimed, it was a wonderful opportunity for fraud. And what a film it could make one day . . .'

'How was the musical morning?' I asked as we returned to the hotel.

'I'm to go back tomorrow. We've only come to the end of the first act. The trouble is that I can't read a score—not that it matters as Preston makes it all wonderfully lifelike, humming and thumping and beating time with a ruler. "Now I bring in the drums, boom, boom, boom," he'll say, pounding the desk, "and here the cymbals." Wonderful work for the fire irons, that. And then, of course, there's the dancing to be explained. He's devising a system of notation which leaves me flummoxed, not that this bothers him. He's completely absorbed and all he needs is a presence.'

Preston insisted that we should stay on in Kaunas until the ship was ready to sail, though we should have preferred to move to Memel. His insistence was a measure of his boredom. There was nothing left for us to explore in Kaunas and the books we had brought for the five-day voyage were nearly finished. The hotel entrance hall, which offered the only alternative seating accommodation, was nearly as depressing as our bedroom. However, people occasionally went in and out and there was some movement in the street outside.

I was coming to the end of our last book, a history of the Baltic States, when our dining companion hesitated as he passed, and then stopped and bowed.

'Dovydaitis,' he said, pulling out a visiting card from an inner pocket.

'Benton,' I replied, but without a visiting card to prove it.

'You must excuse me,' he said gravely, 'but I see that you sit alone for many hours—and that you are interested in my country,' he glanced at my book. 'Your husband is a diplomat? Or a merchant perhaps? Allow me to offer you a glass of beer. It is very light. Or some cranberry juice, perhaps?'

'Please sit down,' I said. 'My husband is in the Foreign Service. May I ask about you?'

'I am a refugee.'

'Then you are not a Lithuanian?'

'Oh yes, I am. I live in Kaunas since eighteen years.'

'I don't understand.'

'My home is in Vilnius, which is the capital of the Lithuanian people. Eighteen years ago it was taken from us. Vilnius was wonderful, a city of beautiful buildings, with theatres and concerts and culture. Kaunas is nothing. You have seen for yourself the best hotel.' He gazed disdainfully at the dusty curtains and the single potted palm.

'But Lithuania has been independent since the last war. How did you come to lose your capital?'

'It was seized by the Poles in 1920. We gained our independence, but we lost our beloved Vilnius. So here I am. You understand now?'

The hours passed pleasantly enough chatting to Dovydaitis. Like many people with a national grievance his thoughts appeared to be mainly retrospective. Lithuanians remembered a glorious past when, in the fourteenth century, their dominion had extended from the Baltic to the Black Sea. Since then, they had been a pawn in the power game.

The Latvian and Lithuanian languages shared a common root. Both countries had a significant folk culture, a sense of nationality and a craving for nationhood, but the fact that Lithuania, under Polish influence, became Roman Catholic while Latvia adopted the Lutheran religion, had created a certain distance between them.

Now, each country was independent and keenly concerned with its own affairs.

Looking back, the time in Kaunas was wonderfully restful. Stresses tend to accumulate, and a time of confinement with nothing to do and no demands on one can be remarkably restoring, provided it does not last too long, and the talks with Dovydaitis had just preserved the delicate balance.

It was a relief to reach the harbour in Memel and see the BALTEAKO, 1,328 tons of sturdy workhorse, tied up alongside the Baltic timber tramps, their decks loaded with pit props. 'They carry a very profitable cargo,' said our captain, Frankie Ayres, seeing our interest. 'If they don't get a handsome return on the pit props, they clean up on insurance for "cargo washed overboard in a storm". Come up on the bridge for a nightcap before you turn in,' he added. 'This is my third seventieth birthday and it needs celebrating.' His precise age had long passed into official uncertainty, but he was one of the most reliable masters in the line, and the company turned a blind eye.

In a corner of the cabin stood an embroidery frame holding a half-finished *petit point* of exceptional delicacy. 'My way of passing the time,' said Ayres. 'At my age you don't sleep much, and I never was one for the booze.'

Five days later we tied up in the Pool of London.

CHAPTER 4

The holiday was a delight. England, though a little shame-faced about Munich, appeared calm and unimpressed by the menace of the German military machine. Sam turned twelve eight days before Christmas and we took the boys to the circus at Olympia, and shook hands with the tail-coated gentleman who swung by his teeth from the high trapeze. Three weeks before, Kenneth had given him an entry visa to the U.K.

The boys were always busy. Sam was methodically sorting stamps and sticking them in an album. Mark, eighteen months younger, had decided with his usual inconsequence to collect only brown ones, and with no special purpose in view. Both boys were happy in my mother's house, where we stayed, and at school. They talked excitedly of the five days' voyage to Riga which they would have to make on their own at Easter.

When we returned to Latvia in the BALTABOR, a vessel from the Pacific run recently converted to carry cargo and the maximum of twelve passengers allowed to a ship without a doctor, winter had clamped down. Snow was falling as we sailed through the Kiel Canal and soon icicles, as thick as a man's arm, were hanging from the shrouds.

As we approached the Bay of Riga a grey line bounded the Horizon—the ice. Winds from the north had broken the edge into blocks and piled them one upon another in a low ridge. The ship ploughed steadily towards it. Out on the open deck we leaned over the rail as the reinforced bows plunged with a grinding shudder into the ice wall. All around us the frozen sea stretched unbroken. Only a darker trace showed where the ice breaker had opened a passage which had rapidly sealed over with a thinner layer of ice. The ship was shivering under the strain, her plates grinding painfully.

'She doesn't like it at all,' remarked a deck hand who was chopping ice from the rigging with an axe. 'Even the breaker can't cut its way through the field. It's duck-shaped and slides up on the ice and smashes through with its dead-weight.'

We had sailed right into the heart of winter and the ice closed behind us. It would be nearly four months before the land was freed again to relax into leaf and blossom.

Riga was transformed under a mantle of snow. When the ship tied up we walked across the quay, round the great Vorburg block of flats and up to our own front door. Lotte was waiting in a clean apron.

The winter rhythm was now firmly established. The chill and apprehension of late autumn had vanished. Oppressive greys had given place to brilliant contrasts—sunshine which cast sharp shadows on the snow and, at night, great stars in a black sky. Sometimes one woke to a deep hush, and a brilliant diffused light filtered through the snowflakes which fell softly to blur every harsh contour.

The Canal, frozen now and snow-covered, had lost its identity and become a small winding valley. In place of the pontoon bridge over the Daugava a roadway was marked out across the ice, sign-posted in the orderly Latvian manner, 'Alexei Berzinš

Aleja'. We often wondered about the citizen who had earned this impermanent tribute.

Sledges had replaced droshkies, driven by the same *izvoz-chiks,* muffled now in two or more long overcoats turned fur-side in, their shoulders covered with short capes lined with scarlet, which flew back in the wind as they drove, standing up.

Sleigh-riding could be an exciting pastime. If one called to the driver to go faster, he would silently hold out his hand. To go fast cost double. Apart from the thrill, there was less time on the trip for the cold to penetrate the musty fur rugs under which one huddled. Sometimes a sledge overturned when the *izvoz-chik* cut a corner too fine and the runners mounted the piled-up snow at the side of the road. The horses' shoes were fitted with spikes which bit into the ice, and the drivers, padded out with heavy cloth and bearskin, seldom came to any harm. Only the passenger sometimes took a painful toss, but after all, he had paid for extra speed, so what grounds had he for complaint? The most dramatic tumbles took place at night, racing home after parties, but the sudden impact of intense cold after the heat indoors sent any alcohol immediately to one's head and acted as an anaesthetic.

As the cold increased, Lotte's soups became richer and hotter. Food in Latvia was abundant and cheap. Every morning a bottle of fresh cream and 250 grammes of thick sour cream wrapped in paper were left on the doorstep with the milk, as a matter of course. Potatoes, turnips and carrots, which had been sealed in great straw-covered clamps before the snow fell, were dug out and sold in the market together with salted cucumbers and beans. Salads had vanished and oil was a rare imported luxury, but there were mushrooms of every kind, salted or threaded on strings to dry. Salmon glistened on the market stalls. There were fresh fish caught through holes in the ice, sausages of every variety and cheeses, smoked eel and tongue, and red and black caviar at 20 Lats (about £1) a kilo.

The Central Market (or Centralais Tirgus, if you were trying to buy a tram ticket) was housed in a row of four converted Zeppelin sheds, handsomely re-fronted. An English connection of the Kruedeners had married Count Zeppelin, who ran through her considerable fortune in the course of building prototypes of his lethal invention. When this was at last successful, it was used against the country that had helped to finance it. Now, at least, some of the fruits of the Armstead money were serving a useful purpose.

With shopping, cleaning and cooking all in Lotte's hands and no job to do, the days were often empty. I decided to learn Russian and to take lessons from the accordion player at Schwarz's Bar, but this would cost money. My salary had stopped abruptly on leaving Vienna and my alimony ceased when I married Kenneth. We now had to live and keep two boys at boarding school on his pay of £500 a year. We could not afford a car, and our margin for extras was slight, but with the help of Professor Pekšens a small English conversation class was easily assembled and this more than paid for my own instruction, as well as various minor amenities. Gilbert and Sullivan's hero was right to congratulate himself on resisting the temptation to belong to any other nation. English is a saleable asset and no literate English-speaker need be short of the price of a drink or a meal when abroad.

On January 15th Kenneth was formally appointed Acting Vice-Consul and we gave a small party to celebrate. In my diary I made a note: '3 gin, 3 whisky, vermouth, smoked salmon, caviar, liver pate, smoked eel. Total cost about £2.10.0.' In those days whisky, after travelling from Scotland to Malta, through the Black Sea to Odessa, up to Moscow and on to Riga, cost people with diplomatic privileges 4/6d a bottle. Gin was 2/3d.

We were still short of essential furniture, and we needed eight dining chairs to be ready in a fortnight.

'Send for the Old Believers,' said Lotte. The Riga Old Believers were members of a religious sect who had been brought to the city from the Volga Basin after the revolution of 1905.

In due course, a pair of flaxen-haired, bearded figures, wearing Russian blouses, knocked at the door. As usual, Lotte took over the operation. Handing them a page from the Heal's catalogue which we had brought back from London, she pointed to the design we had chosen. The price was agreed. 'Aren't you going to write it down?' we asked a little anxiously.

'They can't read,' Lotte replied simply, 'but they don't drink or smoke and they never fail with their bargain.' In exactly fourteen days the chairs arrived. Fashioned of pale ash wood and upholstered in hand-woven tweed, they were perfect in every detail.

In spite of the peaceful tenor of life in Riga an edict had gone out that attics must be cleared of lumber as a precaution against possible future air attack, and some queer objects were emerging. Friends of ours, the Whishaws, whose family had lived in Russia for four generations, offered us two beds, and the K3ruedeners produced a secretaire made in Massachusetts in 1860. This splendid piece of furniture, six feet high, had two wings which opened to form a miniature alcove surrounding the writer. A letter box and a secret drawer were accommodated beneath the pull-down writing flap and the rest of the main structure, and the wings were fitted with tiers of drawers and pigeon-holes. The whole formed a complete mini-office.

We were now becoming accustomed to the cold, and the methods of coping with it. Inside, one was always warm. If there was no central heating, tall Russian stoves, their tiled flanks rising to the ceiling, were placed between each pair of rooms so that both were warmed. Every morning, a large quantity of hewn wood was pushed into the stove through a small iron door and set alight. Great care had to be taken to see that every scrap of wood was carbonised before the heat was sealed in by an iron clapper in the flue. Otherwise, carbon monoxide could seep into the room, sometimes with fatal consequences. For a rebellious serf, this often proved a convenient way of avenging his grievances, though suspects had been promptly executed.

Murray's Guide to Russia of 1849 reassures the traveller, '... the temperature maintained by these stoves over the whole of the Russian house is remarkably constant, so much so that, in spite of the great external cold, there is perpetual summer indoors. No additional blankets are necessary, and no shivering and shaking is to be dreaded on turning out in the morning as in dear old England, when the north wind drives through every sash in the house. We are acquainted with a lady whose feet and fingers never escaped chilblains until she passed a winter in Russia.'

There were other ingenious ways of dealing with the heating problem. Baron Kruedener had described to me how, in his grandfather's time, the chill of the ballrooms in the great country estates was sometimes broken by driving in a horde of peasants whose body warmth would, after several hours, raise the temperature. The result probably smelt no worse than the staircases of Versailles, which were used as casual conveniences. There were some basic rules for survival in the intense cold, one being never to drink spirits whilst out in the open, as this causes the body temperature to drop, and this sometimes results in death.

We learned to recognize the approximate degrees of frost, even without reading the thermometer which hung between the double windows of the drawing room. At $-5°$ centigrade the snow squeaked beneath one's feet. Five degrees lower, and the hairs in one's nose froze. At −20° one's eyelashes iced up and tended to stick together. As the weather became colder the kindergartens closed, then the secondary schools and finally, round about the −25° mark, the university. No-one went skiing for pleasure any more.

Outdoor clothing became a matter of defensive equipment, not choice. Ordinary stockings were insufficient to prevent cold-burns around the tops of one's boots, and an extra, woolly pair was required. Ears had to be covered, and sometimes a passing stranger would rush up and rub with a handful of snow the face of someone showing signs of frostbite.

For expeditions in the depth of winter a single fur coat was not sufficient and one needed a second, reaching almost to the ground with the fur—probably bearskin—turned inwards. Sheepskin coats, cured so that the natural oils remained, provided excellent insulation. A coat like this had been made for me by a small furrier. The wool was a soft grey and the cut stylish, but as soon as one came indoors the warmth brought out a pronounced and unpleasant smell. Any public building like the Post Office, where there was no opportunity to shed street clothing, was a place to be avoided by anyone with a sensitive nose.

Going out in the evening, women pulled long johns on beneath their evening dresses and felt boots over their slippers. All sorts of extra wraps covered bare arms and décolletés, so that the hostess's bedroom looked like some badly organized jumble sale when the women guests had emerged in evening dress. The overcoats of the police and armed forces hung right down to the snow and the bottoms were left unhemmed, giving them an untidy look. The reasoning behind this was practical. In winter everyone was padded out with so much extra clothing that fit was no longer important and one size of overcoat would suit a large range of figures. A pair of scissors was all that was needed to adjust the length.

For those not concerned with its uneasy history or the tensions beneath the surface, Riga was a delightful post. The diplomatic corps was small, and protocol not oppressive. In Vienna the Legation had been run with a diplomatic staff of four, but here the scale of staffing was even smaller. Our own Legation consisted of the Minister, Charles Orde; a first secretary, Douglas MacKillop, and an archivist, Henry Froebelius, who had been born in Moscow. His young brother, Co, was clerk.

The Minister was responsible for all three Baltic States, a situation which was described by a former incumbent, Sir Hughe Knatchbull-Hugessen, in a brilliant parody of the Athanasian creed. Service attachés, Army, Navy and Air Force, were shared out around the Eastern Baltic, the Military attaché, Croxton Vale, being domiciled in Riga. In such a small community junior staff were constantly invited to parties and picnics. Everyone knew everyone else and gossip was a form of indoor sport, colourful but on the whole harmless. This intimacy amongst the diplomatic community was delightful, though it gave rise to many awkward situations when war broke out.

Although Latvia itself tended to be claustrophobic, local society was varied. As mentioned earlier, there was little communication between the Latvian-speaking elements and the British, owing to the language difficulty. The Balts provided a completely different society with a feeling of wider horizons lost, and a nostalgic aura of their dominant past. Sparkle was added by the White Russians who had settled in Latvia after the Russian Revolution and adapted to their reduced circumstances with considerable style. They were responsible for the delicious food at the Hotel de Rome and in some private houses. They provided the gipsy music in the night spots, and a certain reckless gaiety. They were the leaven in the Lutheran lump.

On February 25th, 1939, the three Baltic States signed a declaration of neutrality. This may have helped to ease their growing sense of insecurity but it was unlikely to influence the plans of their powerful neighbours.

On the renewal, until 1945, of the Non-Aggression Pact between the USSR and the Baltic States, Litvinov made a speech in which he emphasized the great importance that the Soviet Union attached to preserving the independence of the three countries. Then came a hint of warning to Little Red Riding Hood from her grim old 'grandmother'. 'This declaration is made in a spirit of sincere benevolence with the object of enhancing the confidence of the Baltic States in the inability of the Soviet Union to remain an idle bystander in the event of an open or covert attempt to endanger the right of self-determination of these States or to restrict their independence.'

In other words, it was clear that any move by an outsider which affected the Baltic States would serve the Soviet Union as a pretext for gobbling up its small neighbours.

On March 15th German troops entered Prague and on March 22nd Memel was annexed by Germany and Hitler made a triumphal entry into the city. A note was sent by our Foreign Office to the Riga Legation saying that in the event of war they would be unable to send extra personnel. Would anyone on the spot like to join the staff of the Legation or Consulate on the outbreak of hostilities? If so, details and references should be forwarded at once. With Donald Gainer, the Consul-General in Vienna for whom I had been working before our move, as referee, my application was sent to London.

As in Vienna, Kenneth was concerned with visa problems

and spent his morning in the public office, but whereas in Vienna the staff struggled for nine and ten hours a day to deal with the flood of visa applications, the Riga Consulate worked only the normal 33-hour Foreign Office week. The Riga Jews, understandably, felt the need of a bolt-hole, but were unwilling to abandon their homes and prosperous businesses and move to a country where amenities were lacking, the climate uncongenial, and the Arabs frequently hostile and sometimes murderous. Many of the richer Baltic Jews owned property in Palestine, as Israel was then called, or had relations there. On the strength of this they would obtain a visa, but leave it unused, returning on its expiry to ask for a renewal. Now visas are supposed to be used for a purpose, not as a form of insurance. The franker clients would explain that what they wanted was '*Bin Visum in der Westentasche*' (a visa in the waistcoat pocket). Others would declare that pressing business called them to Palestine, but that their doctor had forbidden them to travel as yet owing to—and here followed the most remarkable selection of complaints. It was fascinating to discover how many indispositions would allow one to carryon one's business, dine at Schwarz's and enjoy the summer at the Strand, and yet be incapable of doing the same sort of thing in Tel Aviv or Haifa. But as long as the visa problems were just a battle of wits and not tragic, as in Vienna, it was all good fun.

One day Kenneth came back from the office with the news that the authorities had decided that in ten years' time a Jewish Arab state would be set up in Palestine. Meanwhile, to reduce friction between the two races, immigration would be restricted.

'I smell trouble,' said Kenneth. 'Any form of restriction is bound to increase demand.'

CHAPTER 5

Arrangements for the boys' journey to Riga were proving difficult. Air fares were beyond our means and the train journey across Europe, changing in Berlin, was too complicated for a couple so young and travelling on their own. The boat would not only take them straight from the Pool of London to our front door, but with children's tickets and 25% diplomatic discount the return fares would cost only £5 each including five days full board (the price quoted by Baedeker in 1865 for the trip from Hull to Riga by paddle steamer).

Unfortunately, the BALTABOR, in which the boys were to travel, had run aground on a sandbank outside Liepaja harbour and become a total loss, and no alternative reservations were available. This was a bitter disappointment.

However, when we returned from an Easter trip to Helsinki we found a telegram to say that the boys would arrive in two days' time. Easter magic—or a triumph for my mother, who would never acknowledge an insurmountable obstacle to any project which she felt to be important.

The BALTONIA tied up in the Export Harbour and when we boarded her we found the boys in the saloon, settling their drinks bill—ten assorted bottles, mostly tonic water which they had drunk with three lumps of sugar in each glass.

'May I have a word with you?' said Captain Butcher (decorated later, during the war, for bravery). 'They're nice little chaps and we enjoyed having them on board. The mate kept an eye on them, saw that they cleaned their teeth and all that, but I had to beat them once. A deck hand reported that they had stuck their heads out of the portholes and were shouting across between their cabin and the lavatory. Dangerous that. One can't be too careful. Of course, I didn't beat them very hard.' Whatever he did, it had not affected the boys' admiration for the captain.

There was an instant *rapport* between Lotte and the boys. She had planted a date stone in a pot which she kept on the side of the stove and tended most lovingly. So far, there was no sign of a sprout, but Lotte, like many better-known people, believed in talking to plants and we would hear her murmuring, 'Come now, just a little drink. You must grow big and strong because I want to sit beneath you in my old age.' To the boys this seemed a sensible provision for the future, and they agreed with Lotte that the shaggy stuffed dog which spent most of its time on the crocheted counterpane of her bed, should be accorded the rights and privileges of an individual. Communication with Lotte presented no problem, as they had learnt German at Rindseln and, now that they were at school in England, we wrote to each other in that language so that they should not forget it.

On the first morning in the Ausekla iela the boys commandeered a heavy polishing pad which Lotte used to push over the parquet with one of her large feet in its plaid bedroom slipper. They devised a game related to curling that resulted in a lot of incidental floor polishing, a by-product which Lotte was quick to appreciate.

When they arrive in new places children are often slow to talk of their own affairs, their minds having switched over to 'receiving'. From time to time scraps of information about school would emerge, but their thoughts were engaged with new impressions of Latvia, as different from those of their previous visit as my own.

'Where is Jimmy?' Mark asked suddenly one day. I explained that he was in Germany, working in a factory.

'He was a kind man,' said Sam. Mark nodded gravely. I don't think they ever referred to Jimmy again.

The year was poised between winter and spring. The sun shone brilliantly on branches swollen with buds, as yet tightly packaged. The thick layer of ice built up on the city roads during the winter had been cut away, street by street, the traffic patiently bypassing to avoid the six-inch step left by the cutters as they advanced. It would be another month before the parks were filled with flowers, but it was time to plan for summer, which began when the schools closed in May.

Summer warmth was of short duration but the days lengthened until, at the end of June, the sun scarcely dipped below the horizon at midnight. Just as the crops, sown late and harvested early, were quick to ripen, so human activity expanded into the long hours of sunlight and the need for sleep diminished.

West of Riga lay the Strand—twenty-five kilometres of sandy beach fringed by dunes and pine forests. With the exception of the gingerbread pavilion of the old Kurhaus at Edimburg and the hydropathic establishment at Maiori, no building has been allowed within sight of the sea. In the forest behind the dunes were the *dachas*, wooden houses of varying sizes and pretensions in which people spent the summer. A long metalled highway linked the various resorts, while sandy tracks edged with boardwalks branched off into the forest. Each *dacha* was surrounded by a low fence of white palings, and tall pines rose from amongst the lilacs and flowering creepers of the gardens. Everyone who could afford it moved down to the Strand at the beginning of summer, the husbands commuting to Riga by train and the wives passing their days bathing and gossiping over coffee on the shady verandahs.

Now we had to find a *dacha*. With one or two scribbled addresses we set out with the boys for the railway station. The train stopped at Tornakalns and Zasulauks in the suburbs of Riga. Imanta, the station for the race course at Solitud, lay within the official city limits, but after Babite the railway crossed the river Lielupe to Bulduri, the first stop at the Strand.

Instead of flowing north into the sea the Lielupe veers east towards Riga and runs parallel with the beach so that the Strand, for a distance of about eight miles, forms a narrow strip between river and sea, giving the inhabitants a wonderful choice of bathing, fishing and sailing.

At this time of year the Strand was deserted, all the *dachas* silent and shuttered and looking very small amongst the forest trees.

'Darzkopibas iela?' we asked the level-crossing guard. He pointed towards the river. We crossed the metalled road and set out through the deep sand drifts swept onto the boardwalks by the early storms, and cocooned beneath the snow for five months. Here and there a piece of fretting had come away from a gable under the weight of the snow, or a gate sagged on its hinges. It was as if the set for a Chekov play had been left abandoned when filming was over.

We found our address and unlocked the small house, aromatic with the tang of freshly sawn timber. No-one had yet lived in it and the landlord said we might choose the paint for the windows and doors. Although ten minutes' walk from the sea, it was close to the river. The kitchen stove was shining new. There were three bedrooms, a living room, an enclosed verandah and—most unusual luxury for a small *dacha*—a bathroom and a modern loo. The garden was just a strip of forest with the larger trees felled. Around the stumps the first buds of the blueberries and wild strawberries were emerging. We decided to look no further. In a month's time this would be our home, and the boys would enjoy it in the summer holidays.

The boys were fascinated by the Flea Market, as we were too. The market was held in the Moscow Suburb beyond the station, and was a happy hunting ground for junk of all sorts, as well as occasional objects of value—clocks, lanterns, weapons, samovars, ikons and even jewellery. In the same area peasant women sold hand-woven linens and gloves and socks knitted in intricate patterns.

The Moscow Suburb, built, on the site of a fourteenth-century Russian trading post, had been for about two hundred years a refuge for runaway serfs who, if they were not recaptured within two years by their masters, gained their freedom. A serf in those days could be bought and sold—a manservant for 30–50 roubles and a maid for 10, while a child fetched only 4. An agricultural labourer and his family were usually exchanged for livestock, while a skilled craftsman was worth about 100 roubles. Many of these escaped to the Moscow Suburb and earned a good living.

One day we found in the Flea Market a heavy book with romantic Victorian engravings of the Teutonic Knights with their banners and chargers and helmets crowned with heraldic beasts. The boys were impressed to hear that Jimmy was a descendant of one of these legendary figures, but nevertheless delighted to discover that Alexander Nevsky had lured them onto the frozen surface of Lake Peipus so that their horses slipped and fell and the Knights, helpless in their heavy armour, crashed with their mounts through the ice and were engulfed.

At the beginning of May the boys left. They were quite happy to return to school, and the close bond between them spared us any signs of unhappiness at parting. Ten days later a letter arrived from my mother telling of their safe arrival. Sam had been allowed to steer the ship, but Mark was upset because he had dropped the tooth he planned to send me into the Kiel Canal.

CHAPTER 6

Delight in the boys' company had distracted our attention from the worsening situation in Europe. The after-glow of Munich had faded rapidly. 'Peace in our time' was proving the illusion that it had always seemed to us.

The Spanish Civil War had ended in January and the foreign participants had withdrawn, the Germans with a wealth of practical military experience and the Italians with the conviction that the Italo-Spanish feelings of mutual dislike were well founded. The Spaniards, on both sides, had shown bravery, cruelty and loyalty to the opposing causes to which they still held, at least inwardly. The foreign idealists of Left and Right had gone home confirmed in the ideas with which they had started out. Spain, its people starving and its cities eroded by gunfire, was left alone with its mourning and retribution, and the material miseries which we were to share in a small degree when, two years later, we were posted to Madrid in early 1941.

At the end of March, Britain had offered full support to Poland in the event of attack by a foreign power. Colonel Beck, the Polish leader, returned the compliment when he visited London on April 9th. Britain was dipping her toe in the water.

At the same time my sister wrote from Prague that the

Legation was again functioning in an outwardly normal manner. With the German occupation of Czechoslovakia and the proclamation of a Protectorate, most foreign powers, including the Americans, had conformed and replaced the brass Legation plate with that of a Consulate-General. The British, however, continued to operate under the old title and the Germans, for the moment, let this pass.

'Prague is full of German troops and lorry loads of SS', wrote my sister. 'The Czechs, whom we used to find a little grim and officious, are so much more likeable when they're down. They are born martyrs, in the finest sense, quietly dignified and talking of the time when freedom will be reborn. The Buss monument and the Czech war memorial are always piled with flowers.

'We are buzzing with rumours, of course. They say a million German soldiers will march in and buy up all the food supplies. Soap is scarce and the factories can't make any more as fat may not be used for this purpose. Everyone is going on a spending spree. Some fear the depreciation of the Czech crown; others that even if the currency keeps its value, there will be nothing to buy with it. The unhappy Jews feel it is wise to spend any money they haven't managed to get out of the country.

'It can only be a matter of days until the Germans lose patience and insist that the Legation closes. There is very little work, so we knock off at midday and play darts and enjoy what diplomatic drink is left in the cellars. We are down to gin and tap water now.'

On April 29th, Germany demanded the surrender of the Free City of Danzig and at the same time, the Anglo-German naval agreement was abrogated.

In May, the Germans and the Latvians signed a nonaggression pact which was not likely to make either party sleep more soundly, since the Germans had no reason to fear attack by a country with a population smaller than that of Berlin, and the Latvians were too experienced to place much reliance on German undertakings.

The stability of Europe was being eroded like a sand castle which crumbles a little more at each succeeding wave.

CHAPTER 7

In the middle of May our household necessities for the summer were loaded onto one of the vans which clogged the road to the Strand. Life in summer was simple, and non-essentials were left in Riga. As the *dacha* was new and would need all sorts of fittings the tool box was an important item. The heavy curtains in the flat were unsuitable, so we had gone to the Flea Market and bought vegetable-dyed linen. Flax was a staple crop in Latvia and one could always tell which farmers were growing it by the stench from the ponds where the stems were plunged to rot until the fibres could be separated from the pulp. Most farmer's wives owned one of the large looms on which coarse linen was woven, as well as rugs made from strips of rag. Just as they ignored kilometres and referred to *versts,* the peasants still used the *arsheen,* measuring twenty-eight inches, instead of the metre when selling cloth. This was apt to confuse one's calculations.

Even when empty, the *dacha* had a welcoming air, but once furnished it took on the innocent gaiety of a child in a new dress and clean pinafore. Lotte was already planning to clear a little path from the front door and plant flowers among the tree stumps. It was full summer now and the air resinous with the scent of the pines.

A few days later my mother arrived and we went to fetch her at the docks opposite our flat. For years, the sea had been one of the few things that frightened her, but when her life suddenly narrowed to widowhood in a Devonshire village, a spirit of adventure overcame her apprehensions. Although her languages were limited, my mother had a natural gift for conveying her meaning, even to people who were totally deaf, and Lotte and she were soon deep in a conversation which neither of us could understand.

My mother was fascinated by everything she saw. 'I can't understand why the workmen here have to buy water. It's so pure and fresh straight from the tap,' she observed.

'I don't believe they ever drink it,' said Kenneth, surprised.

'Oh yes, they do,' my mother insisted. 'You remember that little shop near the docks, and there are lots more like it. You see men coming out with bottles of water and knocking the necks off against a lamp post and drinking it straight down. They must get very thirsty.'

'Dear Mama,' I said gently, 'that was *vodka*. And those little shops belong to the State Monopoly.'

She was intrigued too by the abacuses used in the Post Office to sell even small quantities of stamps. 'I thought those coloured beads on wire frames were only made to amuse small children.'

'They're an essential part of commercial life in these parts,' Kenneth explained. 'And not so simple to operate either. Personally, I prefer to add up in my head, but here even the petrol pumps wouldn't be without them and the Latvian clerk in the Consulate has one on his desk.'

'The public typewriters at the Post Office are fascinating,' my mother went on. 'I love to watch people using them. Some write in Russian, which looks rather difficult. Then there are the ordinary ones. I suppose they write Latvian as well as English. But this morning I saw a rabbi with a caftan and long curls typing away and, just fancy, the carriage was going backwards!'

'Hebrew, Mum.'

'Of course,' said my mother loftily.

The Bay of Riga, being shallow, freezes over quickly, but in summer the water is at times almost tepid and it is hardly salt. A long submerged sand bar runs parallel to the Strand at a depth of about five feet, which varies very little with the limited rise and fall of the Baltic tide. This bar breaks the force of the waves and provides an expanse of safe water for bathing.

Since the Strand had been laid out in the last century and the plumbing arrangements of many of the *dachas* were of the earth-closet vintage, people often took a cake of soap to the beach as well as a bath towel. Wearing a bathing dress, a really good wash would have been difficult, but the Latvians had kept up the delightful Russian custom of bathing naked, though the whole affair had to be suitably organized. From eight to ten, men could bathe nude before leaving for the city. From ten to twelve the beach belonged to the women, and children under twelve, except for a mixed bathing zone every five kilometres or so. After mid-day, bathing dresses were worn and the beach was free to everyone.

Of course, life could not stop because of the proprieties. The fishermen must carryon with their jobs. The beach had to be raked clear of seaweed, and a policeman must be on patrol in case of need. So although any man found loitering in the dunes during the women's hours was at once arrested and often heavily fined, policemen, fishermen and municipal cleaners were considered temporarily neuter and could circulate freely. At first it was surprising, as one lay drowsing in the sun, to be asked to move over by a man with a long rake or fishing net, but one soon learned not to worry and got used to strolling up to a policeman, tightly buttoned into his uniform, to ask how much longer until the red flag went up and we had to put on our clothes again.

My mother, on hearing about naked bathing, protested that she certainly did not intend to shed her bathing dress. But Lotte pointed out that, if she refused to strip, people would think that she suffered from some disfiguring disease, and that was the last we heard of her protest.

At four o'clock the wives and children scampered off to the railway station to welcome the fathers home, the women often wearing Turkish towelling wraps strained round their ample figures. According to local convention, when the businessmen returned from the city they exchanged their town clothes for a clean pyjama suit. Although some stout gentlemen looked peculiarly unattractive as they paraded up and down with gold watch chains stretched across flannelette bow fronts, one could only applaud the practical good sense and cleanliness of the outfit. If the wearer decided to substitute the jacket only, keeping on his dark trousers and black boots, then the effect was wholly unpleasant.

Further down the line an English family, the Addisons, had made their permanent home in a rambling *dacha* reminiscent of the Cherry Orchard. Old Mrs Addison, herself a third generation Anglo-Russian, was cherished by a devoted daughter, Una.

'My children have to return to England to have their babies,' Mrs Addison told us. 'Otherwise, after four generations, they would lose their British nationality.' The grandchildren were now scattered, but all of them returned from time to time to visit their grandmother.

Mrs Addison had a prodigious memory and told us of life in Tsarist times, when the Strand had been a favourite summer resort of many Russian families.

'My grandfather used to travel from St Petersburg to Riga by *malle paste* for 35 silver roubles. In winter the fare was only 17. Partly taking advantage of the summer visitors, of course, but transport was always cheaper in winter because the snow was soon beaten down to make a smooth surface, whereas in summer the dirt roads were dreadfully dusty or else became seas of mud. That's why the roads are so wide in Rus'Sian towns and villages, because you had to have room to take a fresh track every time the old one became a morass. My grandfather sometimes travelled from St Petersburg with the Queen's Messenger. Those gentlemen had fast carriages and sleighs and they were not averse to turning a useful penny by taking a passenger at £25 or £30—a lot of money in those days.'

Life in summer was organized to allow the working population a long evening in the fresh air. Offices and shops opened at eight and closed about three. I often saw Kenneth off by the early train. After a swim before breakfast we were always hungry and the station buffet looked tempting. If time allowed, we would enjoy a cup of coffee and a croissant. West of Bulduri the line stretched dead straight to vanishing point. 'If you start your coffee when the train is just in sight, you'll have plenty of time to finish it without burning your tongue,' Dick Whishaw, our neighbour, advised us.

Sometimes I too went in to Riga for shopping, and we would lunch together on curd rissoles with a salad of cucumbers and tomatoes in sour cream at an open-air restaurant on the bank of the Canal.

In their leisure hours, firemen were set to spraying the grass in the parks with their hoses. Once more, a practical Latvian idea. The beds were now filled with brilliant flowers, changed as soon as a few petals had faded by the women with the small wooden stretchers.

In this tranquil house-proud atmosphere it was difficult to realise that from the spring of 1915 until peace with the Soviet Union was signed in August 1920, Latvia had been almost continuously a zone of war and destruction, the anvil, as Lenin described it, hammered by both Germans and Russians. If, at times, we were irked by the complacent tidiness of the present-day Latvia we tried to remember that this nurseryrhyme scene had arisen from blood and ashes, and evolved out of chaos.

'The Germans have had Donald Gainer removed from Vienna,' Kenneth told me one day. 'The *Times* says that during criminal trials—the ones we were lucky enough to miss, I suppose—it came out that he was mixed up in espionage. *He* wasn't, as we know. Our people believe that this is a reprisal for the expulsion of the German Consul-General from Liverpool. Gainer is to be Minister in Venezuela, so I don't suppose he minds.'

In the middle of June my sister arrived in a small ship from Copenhagen, where she had been waiting for a boat, and we made up a couch for her on the verandah. She was awaiting a new posting and recuperating after the strain of the last weeks in Prague. The long sunlit mornings on the beach and the free flow of air over one's skin were ideally soothing. Often when the red flag was hoisted and we pulled on our beach clothes, we would lie in a warm hollow in the dunes, too lazy to read, while the small waves uncurled on the sand below and little creatures rustled in the sea grass.

Miggs was enchanted with the hedgehogs that bustled along on the boardwalks, sensibly avoiding the deep sand of the roads. 'They always look as if their socks had come down,' she said. 'Something to do with their thin little legs above their large flat feet.'

On hot afternoons we lay under the pines reading or trying,

in a drowsy way to analyze what it was that made up our happiness. 'Surprise has something to do with it,' I suggested. 'Until your telegram arrived I never even hoped that you might come to Riga. And contrast too—the peace of our lives here after so many stresses. And a sense of transience, the feeling that our time is short—that we are in the eye of the hurricane.'

There was magic in the white nights, when the pine trees threw a double shadow, from the sinking sun and the rising moon. Though the light faded, darkness never came, only a hush and a dimming as the scent of the lilacs became heavier in the moist air. Voices softened and people brushed past one like moths. Quiet figures grouped themselves round a single lamp on a verandah table, the fretted woodwork like lace against the glow.

We had no newspaper deliveries or telephone at the Strand. News came with Kenneth's return on the afternoon train. One day he announced that Henry Hobson, the Consul, had been asked by Radio Latvia if members of his staff would broadcast 'Lady Windermere's Fan'.

'I couldn't even assemble a suitable cast for "Red Riding Hood,"' said Hobson, 'but we must show the flag.' He turned to my mother. 'You'll have to be the Duchess. They won't know over the air that you're far too young looking and not the type at all. You, Peggie,' he said pointing at me, 'can be the daughter— if there is one—and Kenneth, you'll be one of those other fellows . . . I'll be Lord Windermere. We'll soon have the whole thing set up.'

A few days later we were laughing over the glowing reviews in the press. Hobson was commended first, as befitted his seniority, though to be fair, his marvellously unemotional reading of the more dramatic scenes had appealed to the Latvian audience as being typically English and quite admirable. My mother was delighted to find that in Latvian her name became 'Pollock Kundze' Harold Hobson had become 'Hobson Kungs' and Dorothy Corrie, being 'Miss', was described as 'Jaunkundze'.

We had applied for passages in the BALTEAKO for the boys' summer holidays but the answer was slow in coming through. Following attacks on post offices and railway stations a wave of IRA bombs was now disrupting postal services in England. A few days later a telegram arrived calling Miggs to Oslo, and she set off on the long train journey via Berlin, where she planned to visit a friend.

When we went to meet the boys they were leaning over the rail of the BALTONIA. The voyage had been a happy adventure, the only disappointment being the absence of their friend, the negro cook, who had got a part as a slave in a West End musical.

On the first Saturday afternoon Kenneth and the boys set off to look for a boat. A long and rather leaky craft, flat-bottomed and pointed at both ends, was tied up by a jetty on the river below our garden. The owner said he would be happy to let it for the rest of the summer and would have no objection to Kenneth's boring a hole in the thwart and fixing a mast. A whole week-end was spent with hammer and nails while I cut and sewed a rough linen sheet to make a sail. An attempt to attach lee-boards was unsuccessful, so Kenneth arranged with the local carpenter to fit a nine-inch keel, which just about allowed the boat to tack into the wind.

Opposite the *dacha* the Lielupe was wide and the water deep, with the dark translucence of smoked glass. In calm weather our boat slid along quite happily, but a sudden gust of wind would cause the leverage of the mast to strain the timbers so that they opened to allow a gush of water to well up between the planks. One of us was always ready to bail and the bucket was as important a piece of equipment as the home-made paddles.

Nights were getting longer, but there were still several hours of daylight for swimming and sailing after Kenneth returned from the office.

At week-ends we would take a picnic and sail down the river and under the railway bridge, where men perched on the girders jerking for fish, a cruel but effective system. Half a dozen large hooks were fitted to a trace and held against the current by an iron weight. The line was lowered into a shoal of fish, easily visible in the clear water, and then jerked sharply up and down so that one or more of the hooks caught in the fishes' flanks and they were dragged bleeding into the basket. No skill was required, only a certain callous doggedness.

Every time we passed the boat yard near the bridge the owner seemed surprised to see us still afloat. Left to itself, the boat would probably have disintegrated quietly, but we cherished the leaky old craft, the only one we could afford. Around the *dacha* the zinnias had just begun to bloom and the grass had grown so long that Ukermarks, our landlord, had to cut it with a scythe. At night we opened the window behind our bed and the stars came crowding in with the damp fresh air of the forest. On stormy nights we could hear the waves beating on the beach. Each evening before we went to bed we walked arm in arm to the gate and turned to look at the little house with the two giant pine trees tall in the clear night air, the brilliant arc of the plough stabbed out in the sky behind them. We savoured each remaining day of peace, but our minds were uneasy.

CHAPTER 8

One hot Sunday Baron Kruedener drove us to Rindseln. In the days when we lived there and made the long drive to the railway station in the brake, we used to dread a following wind which would keep us enveloped in the dust cloud raised by the horses' hoofs. Now, at a spanking thirty miles an hour, Kruedener's high-chassis Ford could outdistance the summer breeze. The Baroness, Tante Hella as the boys called her, was waiting for us in the porch of the low wooden building.

'Welcome to Rindseln. Here is the *Wirlin*,' said Tante Hella. The stout old woman who used to bake such wonderful bread and cook great dishes of mushrooms in cream and pike with butter sauce, came out of the kitchen wiping her hands on her apron.

'Have you come back to us?' she asked.

'No, but I've brought the boys to see you with their new father,' I explained, and changing the subject quickly, 'Are the hens laying well, and does the fisherman still come?' Once a month an itinerant fisherman would spend the day in the punt and in the evening hand over half his catch, some of which was stored in a tunnel by the lakeside, which was filled every spring with blocks of winter ice.

The boys had raced down to the water and were sitting on the diving board where Anukelchen, the peasant girl engaged to look after them, used to take them every evening with soap and towels for their daily bath. Tello, the old liver-coloured spaniel who had once nipped Sam sharply in reproof when he tried to push little sticks up his nose, was panting at their side.

As we sat chatting Sam and Mark took Kenneth to see the beehives and the privy, which had a drop so deep that we used to wonder how we could rescue them if they fell down the hole.

My mind returned to the sunlit summer of five years ago. 'And how is Fuchs?' I asked. It had been a great disappointment to Baron Kruedener that neither of his sons liked riding, the result of miserable hours spent as small boys on and off the backs of the vicious little Oesel ponies which, as long as they didn't put a child off riding for life, must have made any subsequent relations with a horse seem quite pleasant. So the Baron had no companion on his long rides through the firebreaks in the forest and was delighted when I timidly agreed to ride the former hunter Fuchs, who had now been demoted to pulling the manure cart. In the heyday of Baltic life, before the First War, the local hares, which grow to great size and strength, were hunted like foxes in England, and there were still traces of the bloodstock brought over from England at the time. Fuchs clearly had respectable forbears.

As long as the Baron was about, Fuchs would respond to orders, but I felt uncertain how much I could influence him on my own. Determined to put this to the test, I had told the stablemaster to saddle the horse and bring him round to the back door on post day. So, with the saddle-bags attached, off we went on the fourteen-kilometre ride. Once we were out of sight of the house, Fuchs strolled along the verge, stopping every now and then to pull chestnut leaves from the trees with an agonizing jerk. Things were no better when we left the avenue and he turned to eating grass. Finally he either satisfied his appetite or decided that an afternoon stroll was preferable to pulling the manure cart, and after a couple of hours we were safely back with the mail. Afterwards, Baron Kruedener had scolded me. 'Do you realise,' he had said, 'that if you had met a car Fuchs would have bolted? Cars are so rare around here that unless they go very slowly the horses usually shy. The peasant women out driving just throw their skirts over their heads and hope they won't fall too hard.'

But now poor Fuchs had gone very lame and couldn't even pull the cart. The stable-master had brought out the spring-droshky so that the boys could have a ride. This is a primitive but very practical vehicle consisting of a long plank and two foot-boards running fore and aft between the front and back wheels. The passengers sit astride the plank, which is springy and gives a little at each bump, saving them a great deal of discomfort. A surprising number of people can be crammed onto a spring-droshky, especially if some of them are children. With baskets of food on our arms we used to set out for picnics in the forest, collecting the strange varieties of mushroom which one would normally be afraid to pick. Sometimes we gathered wild strawberries and white raspberries, or all the red and blue and purple berries which carpeted the clearings.

The *Wirtin,* calling to the boys, came from the kitchen with a great jug of the roasted barley drink which, with a spoonful of cream, served as a substitute for coffee, and Tante Hella handed round slices of *Gugelhupf.*

'Do you remember the day when the *Wirtin* gave us soft-boiled eggs instead of hard ones and we had to wipe the children's faces with handfuls of bracken?' I asked Tante Hella.

'Yes, and when we went to pick mushrooms in the fir

plantations you were worried because there was no under-growth, only rows of straight tree trunks and you could find nowhere to—how do you say—spend a penny.'

'And we used to go for walks with Anukelchen and she made us each take a long stick and beat the grass in front of us to frighten away the snakes,' Sam interrupted.

'Quite right too,' said the baron. 'Every year children are bitten by snakes and we lose dogs.'

'But Anukelchen was very silly,' said Mark. 'She told us that the storks brought babies and *we* knew where babies came from, but you wouldn't let us tell her. Look Daddy, the stork's up there now.' He pointed to a large untidy nest on the stable roof.

'Storks are monogamous,' observed the baron, 'and if the wife is unfaithful the stork fetches all the males in the neighbour-hood and they peck her to death.'

'And if *he* has a roving eye?' asked Kenneth.

'The other females are too busy with their nests to care, I expect. That's how life is.' He looked serenely at his wife.

Five years ago I had expected Rindseln to be my home. It was a happy place, but there would have been no freedom to fly away like the storks if the cold closed in.

We were sitting on the verandah looking across the pond towards the orchard where Jimmy and I had spent the night of the midsummer festival with guns on our knees to scare away returning revellers from the ripening apples.

The boys and Tello scampered off in the direction of the stables.

'I'll take them for a ride,' said Tante Hella.

'Come and see what we've done since you left,' the baron said.

The spring-droshky rattled past with the baroness and the boys astride the plank and the stable-master whipping up the horses. They all waved as it turned into the linden avenue and disappeared in a cloud of white dust.

We followed the avenue of chestnuts to the great house on the high ground above the lake. Scaffolding still surrounded the burnt-out shell, and the white columns of the portico were stark beneath the charred roof beams.

'Only a few of the great houses escaped damage during the war,' Kruedener said. 'The best of them were italianate, copies of the work of Rastrelli, one of the architects of Catherine the Great. They were all built of wood and ready to go up like tinder. Sometimes it was the disgruntled peasants, sometimes the Russians and sometimes the Germans. One day we shall rebuild—when the orchards are bearing. We've planted half a hectare already. Come and see.'

We turned towards the head of the lake. The steep banks had been clothed in forest pines, mirrored in the deep water. Now they had vanished and in their stead were naked stumps, like the seats in an outdoor theatre. I stood aghast. The mutilation was shocking.

'We needed cash to plant the apples,' said Kruedener. 'You fell a tree and take the money and it's finished. But the apples keep on coming.'

'Who burnt Rindseln?' Kenneth asked.

'We are not sure. It happened during the German occupation when I was away fighting.'

'What was the occupation like?'

'Not so bad for us. Not good for the Latvians, though. But at least it kept the Russians out of this part of the country. In Livonia, where they set up a puppet republic, there were revolutionary tribunals and people suspected of capitalist sympathies were shot without trial. Life was utterly wretched. So you see, we preferred the Germans, and Ludendorff, who was in charge here, wasn't a bad fellow.

'I and most of my fellow landowners wanted to take a hand

against the Bolsheviks, so we formed a militia, the *Baltische Landeswehr,* but even with the help of some Latvians and White Russians we were only a small force, so we joined up with the German Iron Division, who were freelances like ourselves.

'In the end, our *Landeswehr* came under the command of a British officer, a young fellow called Alexander [Alexander of Tunis]. I believe he's done quite well for himself since then. In spite of everything those were wonderful times.' Kruedener's eyes shone. 'Riding all day and shooting game when there was nothing else to shoot; cooking it in the open or on the hearth of a great hall. Do you know, it was a strange thing, one could go into a ballroom and find the windows broken, the pictures slashed, the furniture hacked to pieces, but all the mirrors untouched. It was an old superstition that whoever broke a mirror would die. I learnt a lot of useful things during the campaign. For instance, I know where the hardest fighting took place and where the tree trunks will be full of shrapnel. Never cut timber like that. It strips the teeth of the saw.'

Tante Hella was coming up the drive with the boys. Each was carrying a couple of eggs tied up in his handkerchief. 'We found them in the stable,' they shouted. 'One of the hens had laid astray. Can we have them for supper?'

'You will stay for supper, won't you?' Tante Hella asked.

'But the boys . . .'

'They can go to their old room after the meal and sleep for an hour or two. It's summer and easy driving at night. What is lighting-up time, Edgar? Eleven o'clock? You see, there's plenty of time.'

The table with its heavy linen cloth looked just as it used to, except that Jimmy's chair was empty. The *Wirtin* had roasted a hare, which she served with cranberry sauce and sliced cucumbers in sour cream, but the boys preferred a bowl of

Grütze, barley baked with milk and butter, crisp and golden on top.

We sat on the verandah with glasses of home-made apple wine. Bats were flickering across the pale sky and the cool evening air carried a faint aromatic scent of resin from the clustered pine stumps at the head of the lake. Occasionally the silence around us was broken by the harsh cry of a night bird or a gentle plop from the pond.

'It is hard to believe that less than twenty years ago this country was devastated,' I said, thinking of the neat houses and well-kept parks.

'By the time the fighting ended,' said Kruedener, 'there was hardly a bridge or a building, or come to that a virgin, left intact. One must hand it to the Latvians. They did a wonderful job in clearing up the mess and getting the country on its feet again.'

'The war in these parts must have been chaotic,' said Kenneth. 'People with entirely different ideas linking up, and then changing sides again, saying one thing and meaning another.'

'Yes, and I'm afraid that goes for your people too.' Kruedener smiled apologetically. 'You may not know that while the Latvians were confidently awaiting the Allies' *de jure* recognition of their independence, the British were negotiating with the White Russian Admiral Kolchak about returning the Baltic States to a future White Russian monarch.'

'But your people were quite happy to work in with the Germans, though you had no intention of allowing them to take over the country,' Kenneth objected.

'As far as the Balts are concerned,' Kruedener said quietly, 'you must understand that we have been here for seven hundred years—centuries longer than the existence of the American nation. Like the Americans and the British, we and the Germans share the same language, but we value our independence, just as the Americans do. In order to try and preserve it we've had to use whatever means came to hand. At least we didn't set out to interfere in the affairs of wholly unrelated nations.'

'*Touché*,' said Kenneth.

It was long after midnight when we reached home and lifted the boys, fast asleep, from the dusty old car. 'We've missed them,' said Kruedener, 'and we miss you too.'

CHAPTER 9

On August 23rd, 1939, the Germans and the Russians signed a non-aggression pact, while German troops massed on the Polish frontier. News trickled through from Poland that the population was calm. Two days later Britain and Poland signed a mutual assistance pact—gilding the lily it might seem, since offers of mutual assistance had already been made and accepted, and with the rapidly growing might of the Third Reich lying between the two countries it was not easy to imagine what form the assistance might take.

'Black caviar has disappeared from the shops,' Kenneth reported. In the climate of rumour and apprehension this seemed sinister, though the Russians might only be holding back exports of caviar to distract their visitors' attention from the Soviet standard of cooking, which by all accounts was very poor.

On September 1st, at 5.30 in the morning, the Germans invaded Poland with three forces, striking in from East Prussia, Bohemia and Slovakia. By midday Warsaw and the principal cities had already been bombed. There was no ultimatum, no declaration of war. The world was simply told that Poland had 'refused the peaceful settlement desired by Hitler and had appealed to arms.'

Britain and France demanded the withdrawal of German troops from Poland and gave a final warning to the Germans. 'Go into Riga, *gnädige Frau*,' Lotte begged, 'and buy some salt and sugar and tea. There is no salt in Latvia. You've no idea what it's like to eat food without salt. When I was in Petrograd in the last war . . .'

In Riga there were queues in all the food shops and at the diplomatic bonded stores most of the shelves were empty. Pounds could no longer be accepted. Everything must be paid in dollars. The exchange rate would be twenty per cent higher than before. In the eyes of the storekeeper, Britain was already at war. Out at the Strand the sun shone with a tranquil brilliance, all the pines red-gold and lofty, with the spiders' webs unbroken in the shimmering air. But in Poland there was death and desolation.

Sunday September 3rd was a still golden day. We sailed down the Lielupe to the sand bar where the river flows into the bay. The boat was very shaky now. Perhaps she would not last the holidays. As we tied up at the jetty we sat in a row on the warm silvery planks and dangled our toes in the water. There was a fortnight of mellow autumn days before the boys need go back to school.

When we reached home we turned on our small wireless set. As Lotte put the bowl of soup on the table the voice of the King came very clear. With our arms round the boys' shoulders we listened to his speech. Great Britain was at war with Germany. Although we had realised that war was inevitable, its outbreak was a shock. All the summer we had longed for the month of September when families return to Riga, the sea is warm and the beach empty, the *dachas* shuttered once more and the small shops closed; when there is a country stillness in the air and the evenings are long and sharp with frost.

Instead, we were packing up the *dacha* and Zasulauks was once more piling our furniture onto his lorry; the furniture which had never stood more than six months in one place. Lotte, running in sudden zigzags, turned all her energy into an inconsistent devastation of carefully laid plans.

When the last room was empty I gathered all the zinnias into a glowing bunch and we got into the hired car which was waiting, its tyres deep in the sand. At our corner, Ukermarks was measuring a piece of ground with an official of the Forestry Commission. I gave him the keys and he shook hands with us and shouted 'Sveike'.

On the way back, we stopped the car at the Addisons' and Una and the old lady came out to say goodbye. The road to Riga was empty, so different from the week before when the families were moving back in time for the school term. On either hand the countryside lay placid and glowing with autumn, untouched as yet by trouble.

Sam and Mark were wearing their grey flannel suits once more after weeks of old shirts and bathing drawers. They sat on each side of me holding very carefully the sailing boats they had rigged. Both were excited at driving in a motor car.

We stopped at the toll house and then the car raced across the pontoon bridge over the Daugava, each section clanking as we passed. By evening the flat would be in order. There remained the problem of the boys' journey home.

For the first few days in Riga we thought we should suffocate. Opening windows only let in dead air from the street. The stars and trees of the dacha had been replaced by the grey mass of the Vorburg flats. Shoes irked one's feet and the pavements were hard and merciless.

In the shops, people were still anxiously buying up stocks. Foreign goods were already restricted. Only one reel of cotton, one pair of silk stockings and three pennyworth of cotton wool could be bought at a time. Foreign cosmetics were vanishing regardless of their colours and scents. Medicines, films, buttons and pins were all snatched up in a panic. Petrol was already rationed, and coffee mixed with twenty-five per cent of roasted barley, but there was still an abundance of dairy products.

By order of the Admiralty the Baltic had been closed to British shipping since the end of August, and the way home now lay through Sweden and Norway. The Orde children had already left, and were held up in Bergen. There were rumours that the town was so crowded that the cheapest rooms cost one pound a day.

The day after the Ordes left came news of the torpedoing of a neutral cargo ship in the North Sea, but people continued to flock back to England like migrating birds.

Terrible accounts were coming from Poland of wanton attacks on the civilian population, of the desperate bravery of the Polish cavalry charging against German tanks, and of the merciless pincer movement closing in on Warsaw. The Polish Corridor, which was formed to give Poland an outlet to the sea, was now occupied by the Germans, who had taken over Danzig. Thornton, one of the British engineers expelled from Russia after the 1933 Metropolitan Vickers espionage trials in Moscow, walked into the Consulate one morning haggard and dusty. He had bicycled the two hundred miles from Warsaw, where he had been working since his expulsion from the USSR.

German attacks on shipping in the North Sea were intensifying. At this moment Miggs wrote that if we could send the boys to Stockholm, the Montagu-Pollocks would put them on the train to Oslo. After that, we would see.

So Sam and Mark flew off to Stockholm waving happily and I went straight to the Passport Control Office to start work. In the entrance hall the staff of the Danzig Consulate were standing disconsolately by their suitcases after their flight from the battered city. On the morning of September 1st they had woken to hear the guns of the SCHLESWIG HOLSTEIN bombarding the port at point blank range. No warning had been given, though the officers from the German battleship had called on the Polish authorities only two days before.

Following the usual crisis routine, the Danzig staff had kept suitcases ready packed in their office, so they piled into the car left behind by the penultimate Consul-General—trains had been requisitioned by the Germans—and set out for Riga under Gestapo escort as far as Konigsberg. The journey went well, in spite of two breakdowns on the Lithuanian roads. They slept in the car and ate only the food they had brought with them. When they finally reached the Hotel St Petersburg they found Burckhardt, the League of Nations High Commissioner for Danzig, who had also fled to Riga.

News came from Miggs that Sam and Mark had arrived safely in Oslo and that the wife of the Legation radio operator had offered to put them up. There was at present no prospect of passages across the North Sea, so perhaps we would like the boys to go to a Norwegian school meanwhile. This seemed a good idea, although school in England was about to begin and the term's fees were already paid.

Riga, meanwhile, had had its first Air Raid Precaution practice blackout and the *dvornik,* our house-porter, had covered our windows meticulously with black paper. People were sending their valuables to Stockholm and we, too, packed a trunk of treasures and shipped them off for storage in the Legation cellars.

On September 17th the Red Army invaded Poland and surged across the country to Brest Litovsk, where the Germans had accepted the surrender of the Tsarist armies in 1917. The roads into Latvia and Lithuania were choked with refugees.

Miggs wrote that the boys had decided against going to a Norwegian school as they felt sure they would get back to England soon. 'Sam has found his stamp collection is getting out of hand, so we have divided the world between the three of us,' wrote Miggs, 'and formed a stamp triumvirate, just in time to stop Mark merely switching from brown stamps to blue. The school has moved to Eardisley in the Wye Valley. I wonder how the boys will find it. Mark is taking things very calmly. He told Sam he had better go on speaking German as Germany will probably be part of the British Empire by next year!'

News constantly reached us of German attacks on North Sea shipping and the boys' onward journey was a nagging anxiety, but on September 25th a telegram arrived from Miggs saying that they had been put on the night train to Bergen where they could take the STELLA POLARIS for Newcastle. She explained in a letter that the Ponsonbys, who were travelling home, had agreed to take them under their wing. However, the North Sea was rough and the boys wrote that after leaving Bergen they had not seen their escort again. The rest of the postcard described the glories of the Smörgåsbord, so evidently they had not been worried by the weather.

From this point, my mother took up the story. The boys had apparently made friends with a man on the train and invited him to breakfast at her club. He, in turn, had tracked down the address to which the school had been evacuated and put them on the train for the Wye Valley at Paddington.

CHAPTER 10

On September 28th news came that after four weeks of continual bombing, on the twenty-third day of siege Warsaw had fallen and the Polish Government had fled to Romania. Once again in her troubled history Poland was to be partitioned. This time, the Germans were annexing the west and the Russians the eastern part of the country.

The war was now in its fifth week and our lives had settled into a steadier rhythm. Papers arrived calling Kenneth for service with the Honourble Artillery Company, of which he was still a member, but the Foreign Office refused to release him and it seemed that for the present we should remain in Riga.

Every morning we walked the length of the Ausekla iela, turned into the gardens and followed the winding path along the Canal, crossing the footbridge to the Consulate in the Raina Boulevard, which opened at ten o'clock.

On the first morning Kenneth showed me round. 'I shall no longer work in the outer office,' he said. 'My room is the first one after Nick's. Next door is Dorothy's office. This is your cubby hole.' It was a narrow little room he had told me about after his first visit.

'Now come and talk to Paul.' Paul's manner was hardly

reassuring, but I was soon to discover that he had an almost infallible memory, which saved me from many blunders. In those days the map of the world showed large pink areas, all part of the British Empire, and we issued visas for a variety of territories, including such oddities as the German and French concessions in Shanghai. So many and various were the instructions for procedure that the sheets were punched and filed in a special loose-leaf book with metal rods a couple of inches high, and amendments were constantly coming in.

On the first morning we arrived well before the Visa Office opened so that I could discover where everything was kept and have some idea of what I was to do. 'It's very simple,' said Kenneth. 'All the instructions are in here,' he pointed to the fat loose-leaf manual. 'Look up every applicant in the card index.' He showed me a bank of steel cabinets.

'There's no need to do that, Mr Benton,' interrupted Paul. 'Not with me here.' In fact, I never found his memory at fault, but the proprieties had to be observed, if only in the presence of the clients.

'See that the accounts come out right, but don't let them get you down,' said Kenneth. The petty cash was handled by Dorothy, but I would be responsible for collecting and accounting for the visa stamps and the money paid for them. 'My predecessor left us a few spare stamps which will come in handy in case your balance is short. Don't believe a word the customers say unless they can prove it, and try not to bother us.'

After this crash course in the duties of a visa officer Kenneth retreated to the private part of the office, closing the door behind him.

At ten o'clock the main door was opened and the clients began to arrive. They were a curious mixture, prosperous businessmen, rabbis with black caftans and long curls beneath their flat black hats, and pale anxious refugees. Most of our business was conducted in German, with occasional broken English. Paul's German and Latvian were fluent and his Russian a lot better than mine.

It was clear that, as in Vienna, a large part of our clientele would be Jewish. The Jews in Latvia formed three distinct cultural groups, the German, the Russian and the Orthodox. Those from Courland and Livonia had officially adopted the German language and their representatives used it in the *Saeima* or parliament. Possibly as a result of the tradition of tolerance fostered by the Dukes of Courland they enjoyed a good working relationship with the Baltic barons, each of whom had at least one Jewish dealer who would come from the nearest town to supply farming equipment and buy up crops, or haggle over the price of timber from a strip of forest which the landowner wished to sell. Many of the city Jews engaged as middlemen also promoted Baltic German commercial enterprises.

'Hitler must be wrong about the Jews,' Kruedener used to say with a mischievous grin. 'You can prove it by simple arithmetic. Every Balt, every German too, knows at least one good Jew. Now if they each know one, that adds up to millions, more than the whole Jewish population, so where are the bad ones?'

The Russian Jews, mostly settled in Riga, had assimilated well, but they took a keen interest in Russian affairs and used their own language in the *Saeima*.

The Orthodox Jews, more numerous than either of the other two groups, lived mostly in Latgale, where they were allowed to keep to their ancient religion and customs. It was they who waited so patiently in our office for visas to the Holy Land, and wrote diligently on the Hebrew typewriters in the Riga Post Office. In the *Saeima* their representatives spoke Latvian.

Whilst the well-established Jewish businessmen of Riga

enjoyed considerable prestige and expected a certain amount of preferential treatment, the small traders from the Moscow Suburb and outlying settlements had always been accepted on sufferance as necessary, but subservient and rather distasteful members of the community, so it seemed quite natural to them that they should be ignored and constantly pushed to the back of any queue. In desperation they would resort to various dodges to attract attention. On the second morning I was disconcerted at being greeted by a rabbi on his knees who seized the hem of my dress and shuffled after me still clutching it.

'This won't do, Paul,' I said. 'We must take everyone in strict rotation. Keep a careful watch and make sure that no one manages to push in out of turn.'

Seeing that the office was to be run on orderly British lines, Paul decided that discipline could be extended.

'I shall call you *Frau Konsul*,' he announced, 'and I shall see that the applicants do too.'

Restrictions on immigration to Palestine were now in force and stiff penalties were being imposed for illegal entry. This made alternative bolt-holes more valuable and, as in Vienna, there was growing interest in all sorts of distant havens. I decided that to show ignorance would destroy the confidence of the clientele, so every morning, before the office opened to the public, Paul would spread the visa instructions along the window sill in the passage and whenever I was at a loss for an answer I would say to an applicant, 'Just a moment, I think I hear the telephone', and disappear into the corridor. A moment or two later, with the facts at my finger tips, I would come back and say, 'It was the Cayman Islands, wasn't it? You will need . . .'

One day, four dirty and dejected English boys—pre-war Hippies—appeared and asked for their fares home. They had been spending a serious-minded holiday in the Soviet Union

71

and found it rather more serious than they expected. Somehow, they had crossed the Latvian frontier and reached Riga. If they had waited a little longer, I thought to myself, they might have been able to study the strange habits of the Russians without travelling quite so far. I explained that it was the Consul who dealt with DBSs (distressed British subjects) and that he would probably advance their fares against repayment in England, if they could find a way home.

On October 5th, the Russians arranged to lease air and naval bases from the Latvians at the ports of Liepaja and Ventspils. Latvian sovereignty, they said, would be unimpaired. Three weeks later they moved into the bases, discreetly, by sea. One saw no Russians in Riga, but everyone was aware that they were only one hundred and twenty miles away.

The Germans, anxious to build up an image of invincibility, announced in the *Rigascher Rundschau* that they had made a film of the Polish campaign called '*Feuer im Osten*' (Fire in the East') and that this would shortly be on view in the principal cinemas of Riga. Advance posters showing burning villages, blazing buildings, terror-stricken women and children, screaming horses and widespread destruction gave some foretaste of the treat in store.

My work in the visa office was a constant source of interest and even the fatigue at the end of a long day gave to quiet evenings at home a special savour. We decided to celebrate our good fortune while it lasted.

We started the evening at Schwarz's Bar in the basement of the Hotel de Rome. The long counter was spread with a variety of delicious *zakouski,* still available from the ample stores of the hotel—red and black caviar, smoked salmon and trout and eel, cold meats, with mayonnaise and sour cream; lampreys, hard-boiled eggs and ham with dill and salt cucumber and pickled mushrooms all arranged on small slices of white, brown or black bread. Vodka was served in glasses of various sizes, each with a special name, and it was important to choose the right one, as etiquette forbade any sipping and the whole glassful must be swallowed in one gulp, followed immediately by a *zakouska* held ready on a fork.

Upstairs in the softly-lit restaurant all the rich yield of the fields and rivers and forests was transformed into the special Russian dishes, chicken *a la Kiev,* salmon *koulibiaka* in a jacket of crisp pastry, *blini* with caviar and so on, which are often so disappointingly imitated in the West. As we sat down to our table my accordion teacher signed to his colleagues in the orchestra to play the Russian romances which I had tried so hard to learn.

Next morning, as it was Sunday, we were idling in bed over the special breakfast tray which Lotte produced as a weekly treat. The wireless set was propped up between us. Already, we were a little nervous of the small black box. We switched it on.

'This is London calling in the Overseas Service of the BBC. A message from Riga states that all Germans in the Baltic States must return to the Reich immediately. Baltic Germans with Latvian passports may opt for German nationality, but they must reach an immediate decision. The Balts will be resettled in Western Poland, which now forms part of the Reich.'

Twelve hundred miles away the level voice went on with the morning bulletin.

We stared at one another in silence. The news was so completely unexpected, apparently the negation of German strategy. Who was behind this sudden migration? Was Stalin seizing his chance, as part of the German–Soviet deal, to root out the close-knit German organizations from the Eastern Baltic? Had the Germans decided that the consolidation of the former Polish territories would compensate for the failure of their long-cherished hopes of annexing the Baltic States? How could Hitler induce the Balts to give up their homes and relative plenty in exchange for an uncertain future in a Germany at war?

The answer was simple. These people would be driven out by the force of their own fear. One word, 'Bolshevik', was enough for those who remembered 1919—the penal island in the Daugava; the mass graves in the forest; the cellars which echoed to gun shots in the night. 'If you stay in Latvia you will be unprotected,' said the morning's edition of the *Rigascher Rundschau*. But unprotected from what? From the Germans' own allies, the Russians?

In fact, the carving-up of Eastern Europe had been arranged with complete precision and embodied in a secret protocol to the agreement signed by Stalin and Ribbentrop on August 23rd, 1939.

The Balts were still an important element in the Latvian economy, and their influence, especially in medical and university circles, was out of all proportion to their numbers. To drive them out so suddenly would cause considerable disruption. And what would happen to the shrunken but usually well-run estates of the Baltic barons—and to Rindseln?

On Monday morning I telephoned to the Kruedeners. The baron hesitated for a moment. The war had not changed their feelings towards us. Did we feel the same? Yes, they would like to come to dinner at once, as they were leaving almost immediately.

All through the day we worked feverishly, preparing correspondence for the Foreign Office Bag to London. There was unrest in the city; stories of trouble in the industrial suburbs across the river. Paul came back from lunch with the rumour that Russian troops were marching in. The day was dank and cold, and grey clouds swept up river from the sea.

The Kruedeners arrived at eight o'clock, he in a check suit which he proudly imagined to be typically English, and she still wearing the dress which had been old five years ago, the hem taken up a few centimetres and the buttons a little more rubbed. She held out her arms and kissed me. She looked thinner and smaller than before and the lines round her mouth had deepened.

This was the last chapter of the Rindseln story. Five years ago, when we had thought that Rindseln was to be our home, Jimmy Kruedener and I had sat under the lime trees and made plans, while the storks slowly circled over our heads. New shutters were needed. We would build a bigger diving board at the edge of the lake. We would put large stones, painted white, along the verges of the linden avenue. We would drain the duck pond and let the deep frosts of winter kill the thick blanket of water weed before filling it again. We would plant fruit trees. Some of these plans had matured. Last August the small estate had been serene and well-tended, with flowers round the house and a pair of young storks nesting on the roof of the stables.

'Some of the apples will bear fruit next summer,' Kruedener had said. 'We have worked steadily these last years and put all we could spare into the orchards. When the apples are all bearing we shall live comfortably at Rindseln.'

And now they must leave, unquestioning, all they had worked for and the very centre of their lives, he bowing to the inevitable and she, dazzled by the mirage of a triumphant, welcoming *Grossdeutschland*.

'We are to be given property in Poland,' said Tante Hella. 'Landowners will have estates similar to their own. Businessmen will take over Polish firms and shopkeepers carry on their trade. The same with doctors and lawyers. It is all being organized.'

'And the Polish owners?'

There was an embarrassed pause.

'Of course, financially it is wonderful for us,' Tante Hella went on, almost as if repeating a lesson. 'They will assess our furniture at a very high figure and we shall be paid for it in marks. They will compensate us handsomely for Rindseln.' Her face clouded. 'If I could take Rindseln with me I would be content. I wouldn't wish for anything better—the old sofa and tables just as they are, and the oil lamps and the saddles hanging under the roof.'

'We shall go south,' the Baron said, 'to the great forests.' He had talked so confidently of having his own forests restored to him when the Germans took over the Baltic States. 'I shall get on with the Polish peasants better than those Germans,' he went on. 'I know the land, and I'm used to working with my men.'

'But can you choose where you'll go?' we asked. They were so helpless and brave and so hopelessly misled.

'We shall be landed at Gdynia,' answered Tante Hella, 'and there we shall be cared for. It is all arranged.'

It was like talking to someone who is suffering from a serious illness. You struggle to respond cheerfully to plans for a spring which you know they will never see. You use banal words to hide your concern.

'How is Jimmy getting on?' I asked.

'He has a very good job now, assistant in a carbon dioxide factory at 250 marks a month.' I thought of Jimmy, so independent when I had known him, working eight hours a day in a German industrial suburb.

'Tell me,' Tante Hella insisted. 'Be quite open. After all, we can speak the truth to one another. Why does England want to take everything away from Germany?'

For perhaps ten minutes we tried to refute the more obvious

falsehoods of Nazi propaganda, but her mind just closed in self-protection, and I regretted having threatened her fragile defences.

At midnight they left. 'Write and tell us where this storm sweeps you,' said Kruedener. 'After the war we'll meet again, perhaps in Poland. Who knows?'

Tante Hella pulled on the little brown woollen cap which used to hang on a nail in the hall at Rindseln. It was shabby when I was living there, but a fresh coat of paint on some part of the old house had always been more important to her than a new hat.

CHAPTER 11

The Baltic States, once a quiet backwater, now resembled an arm of the river which beneath the angry rays of the sun dwindles and turns turgid, while the fish crowd into the diminishing pools, thrashing and gasping in their anxiety.

A growing number of Polish refugees who had crossed illegally over the *Grüne Grenze* (the unguarded 'green frontier' which, before the days of the Iron Curtain, bounded large stretches of every country in Eastern Europe) crowded into the office each day to volunteer for the Polish Legion or seek a visa for somewhere. The would-be legionairies could at least be directed to the Polish Legation, but for the others there was little we could do beyond giving them sympathetic attention and making them feel that they were respected and of importance to someone, if only briefly. When a warning came from the Director of Passport Control that both the Russians and the Germans had planted spies amongst the refugees in the hope that they might gain entry to the UK, our concern became tainted with caution.

The genuine refugees were men existing without hope, just putting off the day when they would be discovered by the authorities and arrested, or deported to repeat the whole process in a neighbouring State. Those who had documents presented them diffidently, as if they belonged to someone else. It was hard to disguise the shock of opening a tattered passport of a prosperous self-confident citizen bearing little resemblance to the man standing before one. Not only were the 'illegals' usually rather unkempt, but they bore a look of deep inner collapse, as if their framework had been damaged and no amount of shaving soap and clean linen would restore them.

As October drew to a close Riga was drowning in a sea mist which blurred the outlines of the city into the grey sky like colour-wash on a soggy paper. The last leaves hung wetly from the trees, their fugitive autumn tints drained away. And through the streets the furniture vans, loaded with the belongings of the Baltic Germans, moved slowly towards the docks. The first German ship was to leave for Gdynia on November 1st. Only the sick would be given cabins. The rest would travel in the hold.

Special arrangements had been made to speed the evacuation—marriage or divorce in two days, instant conveyancing of property and transfer of funds to Germany. The newspapers were full of advertisements for forced sales, and the flea market of the detritus from abandoned homes.

Eleven German ships were lying in the river, tied in a double bank along the quays of the Export Harbour. All but one had been taken from summer cruise runs and their sleeping accommodation was unheated.

As the evacuation gathered pace shops sold out of warm clothing and the Latvian Government closed the jewellers' shops to stem the run on valuables. Rumours reached Riga of a shortage of soap in Germany, so people rushed to buy it up, until they found that they were not allowed to take extra packages with them. Trunks and suitcases disappeared from the shops, as

PEGGIE BENTON

well as the wooden boxes with iron handles used by the peasants. Late comers were obliged to use cardboard boxes which they loaded on to hand carts. As the wharves became congested, baggage was piled outside the dock gates. Furniture and possessions were to follow the evacuees, as well as the money they had been instructed to deposit in the Liepajas Bank for transfer to Germany.

Finally, the once neat paths beneath the trees of the Kaisergarten at the bottom of our road were blocked with piles of crates like the droppings of some monstrous bird. Beyond the trees and towering above them, a *Kraft durch Freude* ship lay at anchor, looking as if scene-shifters had chosen the wrong back drop.

Until now, Germany had been the predator. Austria, Czechoslovakia, Memel and half Poland had been annexed. Now the Germans were withdrawing their kinsmen, but one felt no sense of triumph. The Balts, who had been independent for seven hundred years were now Germany's victims. We watched their anxious faces as they went on board, each carrying the statutory two packages containing knife, spoon and fork, some warm clothing and bare necessities. One sensed the misgiving and the agony of choice between immediate sacrifice and the possibility of yet worse miseries under the Russians. Many tried to change their minds at the last minute, but it was too late to draw back.

Sensing that the mood of the Balts was turning to disillusionment, the Germans looked round for a scapegoat. The Latvian Ministry of Foreign Affairs was informed that a bomb had been placed on the SIERRA DE CORDOVA, which had just left Riga crowded with evacuees. The German Minister set out in a fast launch in pursuit of the ship, which was turned round and brought back to port for a thorough search. A suspicious-looking suitcase was produced and taken to a spot outside the city. The Germans reported that it had contained an incendiary bomb which they had detonated. The Latvian police were invited to view the evidence but could find no trace of a fuse nor any metal parts, only some scorch marks on the ground. The diabolical device, the Germans said, had been planted by certain Englishmen in Riga.

The *Rigascher Rundschau* announced, a few days later, that the Balts from each of the Latvian provinces would be moved *en bloc* to separate areas of Poland so that they could remain together with their friends (but even so, they would still be surrounded by enemies). The houses to which they were going were 'not too badly damaged'—possibly by those who had been forcibly evacuated from them.

The German theatre of Riga was to move to Gdynia (now Gothenhafen) and begin performing immediately. The German school, with all its pupils, would carry on with the term's work in a former Polish school. Each Balt would continue to exercise his own profession unless, as seemed probable, he was conscripted into the German armed forces.

And the Poles? They were to move immediately into the desolate lands left to Soviet Poland. No plans were envisaged for *their* mass migration. No one cared whether they survived. One evening Tante Hella knocked on our door. They had sold everything and were waiting for a summons to embark. Fiasco, the riding horse who had succeeded poor Fuchs, being clearly more useful than two elderly people, had already made it to Germany. Sadly we said goodbye.

In the middle of this upheaval a rumour reached us that the staff of our Legation had left Helsinki, and three days later, that the Passport Control Office in Tallinn had closed. We tried to telephone for confirmation, but the line to Tallinn was dead. The last Swedish ship was to leave Riga for Stockholm next day, and with Sweden preparing to mobilize, their plane service (which, apart from the Russian line, was now our only link with the outside world) seemed in some jeopardy.

And yet, as the last German ship sailed away down the Daugava, life in Riga was superficially placid. Quieter even than before, since owing to the petrol shortage there were hardly any cars on the street.

The Latvians, free of the Baltic element which had dominated them for so long, became almost expansive, and even showed some enthusiasm for Soviet Russia, who chose this moment to send to Riga Eisenstein's film of the defeat of the Teutonic Knights by Alexander Nevsky. At each reverse suffered by the Knights the Latvian audience, usually so stolid, stamped their feet and clapped until the management had to silence them by turning on the lights. Since the action of the film was frequently interrupted to allow Alexander Nevsky to declaim Party propaganda what should have been a magnificent spectacle became extremely tedious.

German efforts at cinema propaganda had proved even less attractive. FEUER IM OSTEN, designed to soften up civilian populations, had aroused so much hostility that managers had been ordered to admit only those with German passports. This reduced audiences to such an extent that the film was withdrawn and an ancient documentary put on instead. One evening at the cinema the UFA German news at the beginning of the programme showed the view from the conning tower of a submarine as a torpedo ploughed its way towards a distant battleship. As the vessel vanished in a welter of smoke and flame the two German officers on their bridge nodded with grim satisfaction. 'Just a fake for propaganda,' we consoled one another. Later we heard that it was the ROYAL OAK, sunk in Scapa Flow on October 14th.

Though German expansionist aims appeared to have suffered a reverse in the Baltic States the German menace continued to grow. On November 9th, the day after the attempt on Hitler's life in the Munich beer cellar, Richard Henry Stevens, the Passport Control Officer in The Hague, was kidnapped at Venlo on the German frontier with his contact Best, and accused of having taken part in the assassination plot. Clearly, Passport Control Officers were becoming unpopular with the Germans.

The same day, Miggs joined the staff of the Air Attaché in Stockholm. In these difficult times Lotte was determined to keep our spirits up. 'England has a new ally,' she announced one morning. Could it be the Americans we wondered hopefully.

'Who is it, Lotte?'

'Ghandi,' she replied firmly and retired with the air of one who had brought a nice bowl of chicken soup to an invalid. The diplomatic corps, never very large, had been reduced by the departure of most of the families. As the work-load on the Legations increased parties became less frequent, but there was a feeling of greater intimacy amongst those under German or Russian threat.

Coffee had now been replaced by the roasted barley we used to drink at Rindseln, and imported goods were no longer on sale in the shops. The shelves of the diplomatic stores remained bare, but with local produce abundantly available as well as vodka and liqueurs from the Wolfschmidt factory, the standard of diplomatic entertaining was maintained. The Washingtons— he was now Chargé d'Affaires at the American Legation—had a pair of Chinese servants whom they generously lent round for special occasions, while the French Minister had a cache of sardines which, for their very rarity, were appreciated more than caviar, which now cost an alarming £2 a kilo.

Work at the office was increasing steadily. Between ten and twelve a.m. the visa clients besieged us, some resorting to forgery, or emotional blackmail, or offers of expensive gifts to achieve their ends. Flowers were the only things we, as civil servants, were allowed to accept, and many of our richer clients went away frankly puzzled at my refusal of a Faberge brooch or a sable coat. But offers like this, though tantalizing, were preferable to cases of Riga *kümmel* or locally-made whisky delivered to our flat, which had to be carried back to the giver by FIX and FAX at our personal expense.

News came that Austrian, Czech and Polish Jews were being rounded up and sent to the death camp at Lublin. Any story like this, and even the rumours which circulated, brought us a fresh wave of applicants. In order to prevent queue-jumping I asked Paul, if I were called out of the room, to make a list of customers as they arrived.

'You must put a little description beside the name,' I told Paul. 'Just enough for me to recognize each one—red hair, thick glasses, small beard, and so on would be quite enough.' Next morning, when I returned from a quick brush-up on the latest visa regulations in the loose-leaf book on the passage window sill, Paul had thirteen clients listed. All thirteen sprang to their feet and advanced on the counter.

'Just one moment,' I said and gave a rapid glance at Paul's list, nicely set on a sheet of lined foolscap and dated:

Rebeka Dukarevics: insipid
Möltler, Mr and Mrs: both awful
Zubersky: nuisance
Pinns: been and gone
Ulfans: ugly as night
Kopelovich: changed into a nuisance
Merlan, Mr and Mrs: quite pleasant
Novik: awful horror

Leznieks: also ugly and short
Schönberg: we know
Smuljans: horrible too
Herr F. Diesendorf: pleasant Viennese Jew, welcome
   on Monday

The only rapidly identifiable name was Maria Fleischner, described as 'smart'. The system had not proved helpful.

Any application with a hope of success, even though this often required considerable correspondence with London, was a relief. Even the people who, hearing that one was kindly received at the Passport Control Office, freely admitted that they came 'to pour out their hearts' and ask for advice on family problems or matrimonial difficulties which were no part of our job, were less exhausting than those one was unable to help.

Frequently I became discouraged, so it was consoling when one day a pot of white chrysanthemums was delivered to me at the office with a little note:

'*Sehr geehrte gnädige Frau,*

   'You will probably be surprised to receive a letter from a stranger, but I do not wish to leave Riga without sending you, through these few flowers, a small expression of my gratitude.

   'I am at home here and my material position and my connections make everything easier for me, but I have had the opportunity of watching how you receive everyone with patience, and so I thank you in the name of the nameless ones, those who have been deprived of all rights, turned out of their homes, whose spirits are so low, for whom it is infinitely difficult to make any request. In the name of these unknown, who have been forced by circumstances to go through the world with bowed heads, timidly, and to whom you, *gnädige Frau,* with your warm heart, have made things so much easier, I thank you deeply and sincerely.

'May God grant that you never learn what it is to be without a home.

'Excuse me that I do not write to you in English. I do it too badly. With my respects to your husband and all good wishes.

Ihr ganz ergebener,

A. Kaplan.'

Herr Kaplan left for Israel and we never heard from him again. The little chrysanthemum survived the long winter and was planted by Lotte in the garden of our *dacha.*

Since the outbreak of war and the gradual encirclement of Latvia the timing of the diplomatic Bag which carried our mail had become much more erratic and this meant an increase in our telegraphic communication with London. Now I was called on to help with the ciphering, a monotonous process which entailed looking up every word in the Code Book, converting it into figures, and then adding groups of figures from a second book.

When similar groups were subtracted at the other end, the meaning was revealed. Someone had to be on call for cipher duty twenty-four hours a day. Nick, Dorothy, Kenneth and I divided the hours between us. Like a doctor, one might be summoned from a party, or one's bed, to unlock the office and then open the combination safe where the coding tables were kept, and settle to 'wrapping up' or 'unbuttoning' a telegram. This shift system meant that our freedom at week-ends was severely curtailed, so any escape from Riga was doubly welcome.

Winter was beginning to bite, but one Saturday the cold relaxed a little and Harold Hobson took us in his car to the

White Lake, a stretch of water lying in the forest beyond the town, where ice yacht races would be held as soon as the lake froze over. Leaving the car in a clearing we walked for about ten miles, crossing the canals which link the stretches of water, and sat in a fisherman's hut to eat our picnic. Hobson had filled a flask with strong vodka cocktails which braced us against the tingling chill. All round us the birch stems shimmered against the grey sky, their twigs a purplish veil across the blue-grey distance. We planned to warm up over a steaming coffee at the inn on the shore of the lake, but when we got there it was shut and the ground floor filled with white cocks and hens, warm and dry but cooped up for the winter in a situation not very different from our own.

CHAPTER 12

On November 26th the Russians demanded that Finnish troops should withdraw fifteen miles from the Karelian frontier with Russia. Two days later the concentration of troops in the neighbourhood of Helsinki was pronounced by the USSR to be an act of hostility on the part of Finland and the Russians denounced the Soviet-Finnish non-aggression pact. The Finns offered to remove all forces but the Customs guards still further from the frontier. On November 29th Molotov announced the rupture of diplomatic relations with Finland, declaring that Russia 'had no wish to violate Finnish independence or annexe Finnish territory, but only to protect the security of the Soviet Union and in particular of Leningrad'. Next day, Helsinki and the principal towns of Finland were bombed without warning, and the Russians attacked north of Lake Ladoga. Petsamo on the Arctic Circle was reported captured, but Russian attempts to land on the south coast of Finland were unsuccessful.

Russia, however, was concerned to preserve a respectable image in the eyes of the world and set up a 'Finnish People's Government' which issued an invitation to the Red Army to come to the help of the 'revolutionary peasants and workers and to end their struggle against provocateurs and reactionary plutocrats'. This notional Finnish government asked the Russians to draw up a pact of mutual assistance with a view to fulfilling the Finnish national dream of uniting the people of Karelia. In other words, instead of restoring that part of the province which had been stolen from Finland in 1920, the Russians were to take over what still remained in Finnish hands.

Two days later, on December 2nd, a treaty designed to remain in force for twenty-five years was signed by Molotov and Kuusinen of Finland, which leased to the Russians the naval base of Hanko, west of Helsinki, and allowed them to buy for one and a half million pounds eight islands strategically placed in the Gulf of Finland. The Russians offered arms to the 'Finnish Democratic Republic' and at the same time launched para-chute attacks, presumably against the reactionary plutocrats of Finland. Finnish refugees crossing into Norway were ruthlessly attacked from the air.

Proposals by the legitimate government of Finland for further negotiations were ignored and the undeclared war had begun. During the long arctic twilight, deep in the forests, Finnish patrols hunted their adversaries with cold ferocity while the world looked on.

One free Sunday we went down to the Strand to lunch with the Addisons. Seen from the windows of the train, autumn and winter combined in a delicate drypoint of bare branches and rustling reed beds, finely etched.

We walked along the beach with the wind behind us, following the spoor of small feet in the sand and the track of a bicycle, wavering as if the rider had turned his head to look at the sea, or been blown off course by the wind. Drifts of crisp shells crunched beneath our feet. The waves were tumbling in, white against the grey sea. And then, coming fitfully on the gusts, a deeper sound. A small biplane with wire struts between the wings was following the shore line, almost skimming the water, flying so low that I thought for a moment it would run us down. It was painted khaki and as it passed two men wearing shiny flying helmets and goggles leaned from the cockpit and waved. We waved back and the plane, with an awkward hop, disappeared over the pines towards Maiori.

Later, as we were drinking vodka in the Kurhaus at Edimburg the barman told us that it was a Soviet machine and that we had been fraternizing with the Russians.

We decided, before the last of our foreign drink ran out, to give a small party, and invited colleagues from the American Legation and our own, the Whishaws, Tom Brimelow, the vice-consul from Danzig on temporary loan to Riga, and Madame de Roemer, a Polish countess, mother of five and a skilled portrait painter, who was hoping to leave with her younger children for Canada.

On the evening before the party Mrs Orde came round with flowers and an armful of precious magazines. I was preparing party food, immensely hampered by Lotte's goodwill, and wondering how to manage, as our wedding-present glasses and party dishes were all in Stockholm.

'I will send round glasses and everything else you will need, and a maid too.' Mrs Orde glanced at Lotte's flushed face. 'You mustn't pay her anything at all. This is a present.'

A few days later, a Polish refugee told us how the wife of Colonel Shelley, the Passport Control Officer in Warsaw with whom we had dined on our way through, had been killed by a bomb as they sheltered in a squalid little village on their flight from the city.

Snow was lying in the streets now and the droshkies had once more been replaced by sleighs, and the flat horseshoes of summer by spikes that bit into the ice.

When we left for the office one morning we found our favourite *izvozchik* waiting for us in the street below. As a skilled man he was given the trotting horses from Solitud to exercise in winter, and the ride was well worth the extra tip. With his flaming red beard and his great body bulked out by two or three bearskin coats he was a magnificent sight. In Tsarist times an extra coat or two was the sign of a rich employer, and a satisfaction to master and driver alike. Until Easter, when the ice began to melt, he waited for us each day. It was wonderful to thrust our feet into the hay piled on the floor of the sledge, wrap ourselves in the bearskin rugs with their musty plush linings, and fly off over the icy roads, the runners screeching round the corners and our *izvozchik* roaring a challenge to the drivers we passed.

On December 12th the Latvian papers announced that the Germans had stopped the steamer ESTONIA on her way from Tallinn to Stockholm and taken off certain passengers. One of these was Gordon Vereker, Counsellor at our Embassy in Moscow, who was on his way home via Sweden. What the papers did not say was that Vereker had been carrying a Bag. We heard later that on the arrival of the boarding party he had thrown the Bag overboard, but as it had not been equipped with the mandatory lead weights, it floated and was picked up by the Germans.

By now, the Finns had withdrawn from Petsamo on the Arctic Circle and settled into defensive positions on the Mannerheim Line. North of Lake Ladoga, the Red Army was said to be experimenting with 'asphyxiating gases'. The Russian Air Force was engaged in intensive, but not very accurate, bombing of Hanko, while the navy was blockading the Gulf of Bothnia which separated the southern part of Finland from Sweden. Our efforts to clothe the Polish refugees not having been successful, it was now decided that the ladies of the Legations should sew for the Finns.

News sometimes trickled through from the Balts evacuated to German Poland, though to our distress there was no word from Tante Hella. 'It was wonderful,' wrote one particularly insensitive Baltic *Hausfrau* to a former neighbour in Riga. 'When we arrived everything was ready in the house, beds made and food in the cupboard and even a kettle boiling on the stove.' The former owners, evicted at a moment's notice from their home, had presumably trudged away, empty-handed, through the snow.

But all letters were not so ecstatic, and as the German censorship tightened up, messages became cautious and cryptic. One drab little postcard was signed in Russian, *'Zhivoi Trup'*, or living corpse. Another said, 'I wish I could be with Cousin Ernest now.' Cousin Ernest had died a few weeks before. The British Club in Riga was old-established and very popular with the British residents, though not with their wives.

On the first Thursday of every month the members met for dinner, which was rich and excellent. Behind each chair stood a waiter ready to replenish the *Kurländer*, or king-size vodka glass, set before each member. Once a year the wives were invited to a dinner consisting of hash and a rather negative pudding. Whether the motive for this was economy of club funds, or an ostrich-like belief that the wives would think they were missing nothing at the other meetings, was never clear. Since the supply of vodka on ladies' nights was strictly limited, the whole festivity was in a low key and the men went away relieved that it was over for another year, while the wives resented even more the makeshift meals most of them ate on the other eleven occasions.

On the outskirts of Riga there was a small zoo where two of the more popular exhibits were an English fox terrier and a Hereford bull. One lunchtime, on the way there, we saw approaching us through the trees, a strange beast drawing a snow plough.

'Is it? It can't be . . .' I said to Kenneth. But it was. A camel, which the thrifty Latvians could not bear to see idle, was swaying towards us, planting its great splayed feet with an air of extreme distaste on the newly fallen snow. Apart from the risk of frostbite and the camel's reluctance to use them, his feet were as well adapted to soft snow as to the sand for which they were designed.

Christmas was approaching, and for a time our anxieties were dissipated. The sleigh horses, their blue blankets flying and the strings of bells on their harness jingling wildly, raced one another spontaneously, regardless of what deal the passenger might have made with the *izvozchik*. The women who swept the lawns in summer now used huge wooden scrapers to push and pile the snow. The policeman opposite Schwarz's stood on duty between two tall Christmas trees, while someone had put a stuffed reindeer in the police box at the interception of the Aspasia Boulevard and the Kalku iela, the main shopping street. The sentries outside the old Russian barracks were now dressed in bearskins right down to the toes of their *valenki*, the felt boots which peasants pull over the rags used to bind up their feet in winter—and which other people wear over their shoes in very cold weather.

In the square by the Russian church a Christmas Fair was in full swing. The pale blue booths were bright with painted toys and spicy cakes and twinkling lights. Opposite them, a forest of Christmas trees glistened under a light powdering of snow. We bought a little one and took it home.

None of our Christmas mail had arrived, since the Bag bringing letters from home was lost. As the prospect of returning to England dwindled and communications became worse, letters from home were even more precious.

On Christmas Eve we made a detour past the Castle and walked along the bank of the Daugava to the office. The sun was just rising, filling the air with soft pink light and all the spires of Riga glistened green and bronze like the necks of a flock of doves.

At lunchtime we closed the office and hurried off to finish our Christmas shopping. By three o'clock it was dark, but the lights caught the frost spangling the trees of the boulevards and the icicles fringing the eaves to provide Christmas decorations much more brilliant and appealing than the cardboard stereotypes used in our cities today.

In the evening we put the boys' photographs beside the tree, lit the candles and exchanged presents—this to please Lotte, who was accustomed to the Continental timing of the Christmas ritual.

Lotte had remembered my mother's lesson in making bread sauce for the turkey, but she couldn't resist enlivening it with pickled cabbage and gherkins in sour cream. To cheer our grass-widower guests we opened the last two bottles of champagne, which sparkled against the small scarlet tulips, lilies of the valley and golden stars on the table.

In the evening there was a party at the American Legation where some of the guests attempted a Cossack dance, while the Japanese sat and played mahjong with hushed concentration. By the end of December the Finns were holding the Russians on the Mannerheim Line. Finnish HQ at Rovaniemi reported that they had destroyed two Russian divisions, but Finnish towns were suffering heavy bombardment from the air. The indomitable Finnish women were joining the Lotte Svard Brigade, which took on all sorts of auxiliary duties and even fought alongside the men. Volunteers from all over the world were going to the help of the Finns.

As a small token of solidarity from the British in Latvia, the car which had brought the staff of the Danzig Consulte-General to Riga was sent off to Finland to help with the war effort. The Baltic States, still eerily inviolate, declared once more their neutrality. With so much suffering all around us, a sense of unreality tinged our feelings of guilt. It was like looking through a sheet of glass at people struggling desperately against a high wind, the effects of which one could see but not feel.

My sister had sent us from Stockholm a *Julbock,* the Christmas goat of pagan origins, twisted from a handful of straw and equipped with horns, a beard and a tail. He was quickly involved in a dark complicity with Lotte, who retired on New Year's Eve to make her usual magic. The *Julbock's* influence was benign, however, as instead of piles of skulls, corpses and effigies of death which she generally saw on these occasions, Lotte announced that in a dream Sam and Mark had come to wake her, dragging an enormous castor oil tree whose branches were sprouting with a wealth of three leaves. Next day the lost Bag arrived with all our Christmas mail. It had been in Berlin. We decided not to eat the box of chocolates it contained.

CHAPTER 13

In the first weeks of January 1940 the thermometer dropped to –30°C (fifty-four degrees of frost by English reckoning) and the streets were empty of children. On Saturday afternoon we took a bus to Milgravis. It was so cold that although there was a full load of heavy-breathing passengers, ice was standing a quarter of an inch thick on the inside of the windows. We turned back and made for home, but within twenty-four hours, following a warm wind from the south, the temperature had risen above zero Centigrade. Water ran in the gutters and as the milder air hit the chilled masonry of the buildings they became coated with a thick jacket of frost so that the whole of Riga looked like a prize exhibit in a confectioners' competition.

After the cold of the preceding days it felt positively balmy and people relaxed and walked briskly, sniffing the milder air, but by evening the roads were smoothly glazed with ice, so that little boys got out their skates and darted about, adding to the hazards of the slippery surface.

The new year started in confusion. The Germans had told the Swedes that they would shoot down any plane carrying Polish passengers, but Russian planes would accept Poles provided they had obtained permission to travel from the German

Legation. International relationships were becoming incalculable. The Russian troops continued to be confined within the base at Liepaja, not out of consideration for Latvian feelings but in order that they should remain unaware that the local standard of living was so much higher than their own. Penalties for a service man seen talking to a Latvian were severe, nevertheless a story was going round that a Russian soldier had asked a Latvian worker whether he was able to buy as much food and clothing as he wished. When the man declared that he could, the Russian replied, 'Oh, I see that you have to put up with the same beastly propaganda as we do.'

By the beginning of February the cold, the most severe within living memory, was so intense that the Baltic froze over and it would have been possible to walk across the sea to Stockholm—a distance of three hundred miles. Refugees fleeing over the ice from Finland to Estonia were hunted down by Russian planes and machine-gunned, or bombed and drowned as the ice broke beneath them.

At these low temperatures one is conscious of the fragility of human life. The cold induces drowsiness and it is tempting to fall asleep and never wake up. Either one must be cocooned in wraps or keep constantly on the move. Out of doors, energies are concentrated in an effort to get from A to B. People walk hunched up and drawn into themselves and the world seems to narrow down to the tiny will to live in each individual.

Canadian visas for the de Roemer family had been granted and the Countess set out with the three younger children, telling her husband that by the time he reached Quebec she would have found sitters for her portraits and there would be money waiting.

We met the Count one day as he was leaving the Legation. 'Come down to Rezekne next Saturday and spend the night,' he called. 'It is five hours by train and we will meet you at the station. Put on your warmest clothes. You won't need to undress. I shall expect you on the Pskov express.'

As we reached the Moscow Station the train bell was already clanging and the engine muffled in a cloud of steam. Peasants were shouldering their way on to the train, which smelt stiflingly of badly-cured sheepskin, home-made sausage and stale clothing. Rezekne was situated near the Russian frontier with Latgale, the most primitive of the Latvian provinces.

We settled with our books and sandwiches on the hard third-class seat. The railway lines connecting Riga with the west were of European gauge. Those running eastward conformed with the broader Russian gauge. The few extra inches gave the rolling-stock a pleasant roominess, but in the case of the slow trains, little extra comfort, since the plywood seats lifted up to allow bundles to be stowed in the enclosed space underneath. Each time a passenger entered or left the usually congested carriages everyone had to stand up while the seat was lifted. Fortunately, our train was an express and only stopped between stations.

Owing to the bitter cold, fuel consumption had risen alarmingly, and as coal could no longer be imported, the trains were running on peat. So, every few hours they had to stop and fill the tender and then get up steam once more. Even the small compartment at the end of each carriage which used to hold a supply of coke for the stove, was now stacked with peat.

The lower part of the windows soon frosted over with fantastic patterns which sparkled in the sun and gradually turned dim and blue as darkness drew down.

As we climbed out of the train at Rezekne the thermometer on the platform showed −41°. Curiously enough, Fahrenheit and Centigrade meet at this point and the readings are identical.

Inside the crowded waiting room we found de Roemer, bizarre amongst the bearded peasants, with his lean and mournful crusader's face and drooping moustache, his long sheepskin coat like some heraldic garment.

'I have brought you two bearskins. You will need them, and a piece of rope to tie round your waist.'

We were already wearing many layers of clothing, topped by my smart sheepskin and Kenneth's fur-lined overcoat, a *papacha* for him and in my case, a fur-edged hood. Out in the yard Christophe, the elder boy, was holding the horse which was to draw our sleigh, a sort of rough-hewn double bed on runners, filled with straw on which one lay covered with what looked like a pile of slaughtered sheep.

De Roemer pushed the rucksacks under the driving seat.

'*Pas assez de place? Mais c'est pour toute une famille.*' Like the cosmopolitan aristocracy of Tsarist days the de Roemer family talked French amongst themselves. What had been an affectation was to prove an invaluable aid to refugees on their way to French Canada.

A room had been booked for us at the hotel, but de Roemer suggested that it would be more amusing to go out to the estate, if we were not afraid of a little discomfort.

'It's primitive, even dirty, at Janopol and we have made no preparations, but that doesn't matter. You can return to Rezekne to sleep if you wish.'

The horse moved quickly, shaking off the deadly cold. As we drove down the main street I searched for any trace of beauty. They have nothing to fear in Canada, I thought. No prairie town could be uglier than this.

Soon we were out in the country, silent and featureless in a pervading frozen mist. One big star hung overhead where the sky was clear. From time to time the sledge gave a leap forward then pulled up abruptly. One's head jerked forward, the horse's haunches strained agonisingly to get the heavy vehicle moving again, and then it toiled on.

'Only a depression in the snow,' explained de Roemer. 'At the beginning of winter they are just small hollows, but each sledge scoops out a little more snow and by the spring they may be several feet deep.'

The journey seemed to stretch into a numb eternity. When de Roemer pointed to a darker streak in the mist and said, '*La forêt*,' it required an effort of will to seem interested.

And then the track forked off into an avenue of ghostly trees, skirted a barn with a fallen roof, and passed a huge pile of stones. De Roemer waved his whip. 'That was once the mill.' All the buildings which, with their many functions, had made the great estate as self-sufficient as a village were now neglected or ruined.

'*Voilà* Janopol.'

A great house, built of wood in the Palladian style, stood pale and silent in the faint light of the rising moon. All over the Baltic States one came upon the classical beauty of such houses, variations in miniature of Tsarskoe Selo. Some had been turned into schools or sanatoria. Others still sheltered the owners who struggled to maintain a few rooms inside the main fabric. Empty ballrooms served to replace lost store houses, or even to shelter the hens in winter.

'During the cold months we live in one room and use the old servants' entrance,' explained de Roemer. The door opened and a girl of about sixteen appeared, her face lit by a small oil lamp. Long fair plaits hung down over her sheepskin waistcoat and her leather belt was studded with brass nails.

'My daughter Jola,' said the Count. 'Is there anything to eat?'

'*Mais oui*, Papa.'

The girl curtsied shyly and hurried to brush us down so that the snow should not melt with the warmth of the fire into our felt *valenki* and then re-freeze.

'*Entrez, entrez.*' De Roemer held up the wavering lamp and showed us into the kitchen. Three narrow beds lined one wall. The air was pungent with the smell of leather and wood smoke. As high as a tall man could reach the walls were studded with the accretions of years of creative family activity—whips made from roe's feet, ozier baskets, spurs, ikons, wooden whistles, peacock's feathers, a bundle of maize cobs, stirrup leathers, a rosary and shelves of books. In one corner a cupboard of blackened wood held crockery and cooking pots. A cracked jug and basin stood on a chair beside it. Hiding one of the beds—Jola's we supposed—was a sixteen-panelled screen painted in black and terra cotta.

'I made this myself,' said de Roemer. 'Each panel holds a fleur-de-lis. *Ici le lys de France. Ici le lys de Florence.*'

The idea had come to him from the illustrations of historic tiles in a book on Belgian church architecture. 'Look, I will show you.' He lifted a small leather-bound volume from the shelf, brushing away the dust to reveal the title.

'Each of these designs is different. When I could find no more I invented them myself.'

On the other side of the screen each of the panels showed an animal surrounded by a pattern of dull green leaves. The beasts had a naïve and secular jollity, particularly the waddling bear and a bitch with a dozen stylized teats to add to her armorial grace.

'Come, I will show you the house,' said de Roemer. 'But it's sad. It's desolate now. You will see.' He turned up the wick in a small china lamp, lit it and led the way up a narrow service staircase. The cold struck one like a blow.

We were in a large bedroom with an open fireplace and a massive chimney breast graven with a coat of arms and the motto *'J'y suis, j'y reste.'*

'I carved that motto myself, using a nail. I just scratched away at the stone.' It was a primitive but effective technique. In one corner of the room was a four-poster of fluted mahogany with curtains of patterned blue and white. Beside it, a curiously shaped majolica stove, a piece of equipment from the eighteenth century, installed long before the Victorian anachronism of the baronial fireplace.

'You see, the room is stripped bare now . . .' But small objects were crowded on the dressing table. He pointed to a coffin-like chest, six feet long and two wide. 'I had this made. There are six altogether. We can pack them and take them with us, and if we have no beds we can use these instead.' He ran his hand over the smooth wood. *'Comme lit c'est parfait.'*

In the dining room another stone chimney piece clashed disagreeably with the eighteenth century elegance of the delicately stuccoed ceiling. Here and there the lamplight caught a pane of coloured glass let into the windows, an ecclesiastical accent which blended as uneasily with the classic Palladian house as de Roemer's rigid asceticism with his wife's cosmopolitan temperament.

In another room he had assembled a small museum of shells and stones, bird's eggs and curious things found. Rows of jugs and pots lined the shelves—a collection of earthenware of Latgale, some simple and beautiful, some crude, some amusing like the jug which whistled for more beer. In one corner of the room a pile of grain spilled across the floor.

'Why does one collect all this? I don't understand the craving for ownership. It is a difficult subject—*du point de vue métaphysique, vous comprenez*. We must discuss this later when we have more time. See all these jars. I collect them, and at the same time I kill them. When a thing is withdrawn from real life it is dead. Look at this belt. I bought it from a peasant, but he should be wearing it, not me.'

'But the peasants are selling their beautiful old things to buy new. They no longer want to wear them.'

'Yes, the present generation has lost the light. They have no faith. Children no longer even believe in the authority of their parents.'

'But nor do I.' De Roemer looked startled. 'I believe in my *responsibility*. Any authority which I have comes from my children's belief that I am searching, with them, to find the right way in life. It seems to me that the accident of parenthood gives no automatic right to obedience.'

'But Madame, what you say is wrong, absolutely wrong.' De Roemer held the lamp high above his head and the deep lines from nose to chin were carved in shadow. 'The authority of the parents is laid down in the Bible. But in Europe today there is chaos. Family life is no longer stable. Some children cannot even distinguish between the authority of the father and of the mother.'

We were in the hall. He bent, drew the heavy iron bolts and opened the big front doors onto the portico. Three feet of snow had piled up against them and an even colder air swept in. 'We used this entrance door once . . .'

Figures of knights on prancing horses cut out of black sheet iron were fixed to the walls of the hall. 'Weathercocks made by my father,' de Roemer explained. Beside the door stood an immense chest, large enough for four men to lie stretched out side by side on its floor.

'In the old days there were two of these, but the Bolsheviks took one. Perhaps they cut it up for fuel, but it just vanished, with everything else that was movable in the house. Not a spoon, not a book remained. When I returned after the war I had to start from the beginning. But I was young then. Now I am too old. I couldn't begin all again.' Canada was too distant, and his arrival there too problematical, to be envisaged as a fresh challenge.

We were walking along a dark passage. The flickering light of the lamp showed at one point emptiness above our heads and the distant rafters supporting the roof. A door from some upstairs room opened abruptly on this gulf. An eighteenth century oubliette, I wondered, or some damage that was never repaired. But I was too chilled to delay our progress by asking for an explanation.

De Roemer opened a cupboard in the wall. Inside were rows of dust-covered bottles, some holding only strange dregs. 'Schnapps and liqueurs which I make myself,' he explained. 'Some are precious. The best is made from a young viper. You catch him in the forest in March and leave him for a week in a bottle to starve and purify himself. After that you wash him in salted water, being careful to keep him alive up to this point—a dead snake is absolutely useless. Then you cover him with 80% spirit and cork him up. The flavour is very delicate. How can I describe it? There is a hint of fish, of earth, of putrescence, in fact, *un bon petit goût de serpent.* I had the recipe from an old Jesuit father.'

But the precious serpent in his bottle was now in the basement of the Legation in Riga, packed up with other special treasures for transport to Canada. 'But I have mixed some into the schnapps you will drink tonight to give it a more interesting flavour,' said de Roemer consolingly.

Back in the kitchen we found that Jola had been busy. A pile of wizened boiled potatoes filled the centre of the table. Beside them was earthenware bowl of chopped fried bacon mixed with scraps of blackened onion, part of a large home-made loaf occupied a wooden platter, its texture heavy and sodden. De Roemer tapped it. 'Jola made this, but it hasn't turned out quite right.'

Jola hurried in with a bowl of cold crackling and a dark, stringy piece of sausage. There were several enamel plates and a couple of forks and some knives.

'Sit down on this bed, Madame. Monsieur too. It is the most comfortable. I shall sit on the other one.'

The two children perched on stools, the lamp with its improvised shade casting a broken shadow across the table. De Roemer bowed his head and crossed himself. The children's heads bent too and their worn young hands followed his gesture. 'Help yourself, Madame.' De Roemer pushed some potatoes across the table. 'You can peel them with your fingers. Take some bacon. We smoke it ourselves. We buy hardly anything but sugar and salt.'

This was real food, the fruit of hard labour, and satisfying after work. So we helped ourselves to the potatoes and ate them with the charred onions and salty hot bacon, and from the rows of dusty bottles de Roemer poured glass after glass of schnapps. 'That is wormwood which grows in the garden. This one is *zubravka* sent by my aunt from Poland. It is the favourite grass of the buffaloes.'

The schnapps ran in aromatic fire right through one's veins and up into one's brain, lighting little flames of awareness and sharpening the hunger that had been deadened by fatigue. The two children ate quietly, watching us with large eyes. '*Oui Papa. Non Papa. Mais si Papa.*'

'And now we'll have some tea—not China tea but wild rose hips.' Here was self-sufficiency, purposeful and constructive, not the hampering autarchy practised by the dictators. The earth and the animals living from the earth supplied the basic wants of Janopol—and many of the graces too: preserves made from wild berries, bright vegetable dyes, soft wool combings for the loom, leather maturing from year to year and serving the family with an almost animal fidelity; pungent grasses, fine-grained woods, and flax for weaving the household linens.

The brass nails in Jola's belt gleamed dully.

'What a beautiful belt. Did you make that too?'

De Roemer bent down and pulled a small chest from under the table. Tools were fitted in rows round the sides and graded nails lay in little boxes one above the other. He lifted out a block of wood dented with the impress of hollow metal studs, and a pair of dividers.

'You see, this is sole leather. One cuts a long strip, then takes the dividers and marks the intervals so. Then one pierces a hole, slips through it the double shaft of the stud, cuts it and hammers it down on this block. These nails are pure brass. One can't buy them here. My wife brought them from Belgium. And look what the children have done today.' He pointed to a stencil of an R surmounted by a coronet. A row of potato sacks with the design painted op them in black hung from a rod balanced across the open cupboard doors.

In the small circle of light thrown by the lamp Christophe's fair head was bent over a piece of wood which he was branding in a formal pattern with a thin poker thrust into the glowing fire on the hearth. The smooth wood shrank and hissed under the searing iron and small puffs of acrid smoke brought tears to the boy's eyes.

'The evenings are long in the country. One uses one's hands. *On réfléchit.*' De Roemer showed us brushes made by Christophe with hair from the horses' tails, and mittens knitted in traditional patterns by Jola. Then he brought out a bundle of photographs showing copies which his wife had made, throughout the length and breadth of Poland, of portraits of de Roemer ancestors, some miniatures, others life-size.

'Twenty years' work.' He looked at them sadly. 'I wonder if any of the originals will survive.'

We glanced at our watches. It was ten o'clock.

'It is time to go back to Rezekne.'

'Why? Stay here if you are not afraid of the cold. Take our beds. We will lie down in the next room.'

To protest that they would suffer hardship sleeping on the floor at an indoor temperature of –20°C was unavailing.

'Hunger and cold are no longer important to us. If the children feel the cold it is an experience for them.'

So Jola found somewhere two sheets, the colour and texture of brown bread. A couple of extra sheepskins were thrown on the beds and the flickering light beneath the door of the next room showed that the family was settling down for the night. As we stripped off our boots and coats there was a timid knock and Jola's face appeared in the doorway. 'I am afraid you will not be able to sleep Madame. Our beds are so hard.' She picked up her father's glasses and his rosary. 'We shall be going to mass at eight tomorrow morning. Do you mind if we wash our faces in here? There is only one basin and jug.'

The fire had died down and we could see our breath, filmy in the light of the candle. My bed was made of planks covered with old sacks from which the straw had oozed in places, leaving just thin hessian over the wood.

Next morning the jug was only half full of brownish water, scummed so that I thought it had come from the slop pail. Water was precious because at this temperature all sources of it were frozen solid, and it needed an axe to chop ice which could be melted down.

As we got ready the family drifted in and out. I found a mirror, smaller than a saucer, and propped it up to give a mottled reflection. De Roemer picked up a comb and ran it through his drooping hair.

'We don't eat anything before mass,' he told us. 'Afterwards we will go to the hotel and meet you there.'

Two sledges were waiting by the door, the double bed of the night before and a small two-seater with up-sweeping prow, pulled by the mother of the other horse and driven by Jola. By the time the red brick towers of the church appeared the cold had bitten through all our felt and sheepskin. Jola, struggling to control the older horse, stopped from time to time to rub her cheeks. 'My face freezes so easily,' she said.

The horses were tied up in the churchyard and we wandered down the wide ugly street looking for the Hotel Casino. The dining room was empty and the shabby waiter told us that there were no eggs, but when the others arrived we could have bread and coffee and fried ham.

After nearly an hour the de Roemers appeared.

'We have ordered some coffee and there is ham.'

'*Merci, non.* We will eat nothing. I have a piece of bread here.' He slapped the pocket of his sheepskin coat. But the coffee was already steaming on the table, and the waiter brought the ham, so w.e were spared further argument, and the children's cheeks lost some of their pallor.

About half past ten we went down to the frozen lake. Races had already begun, six sledges at a time round a circular track marked out with broken fir branches and numbers scrawled on pieces of cardboard. Officers in uniform shouted instructions from a rough-hewn stand. Small sausages and hunks of bread, and thick glasses of vodka, were being sold from an improvised buffet.

Friends and backers of the racing drivers, muffled in sheep-skin, bulged against the ropes on the edge of the track. Bearded *staroveri*, the horse traders of the district, flicked their whips and paced their animals up and down. 'All these horses work in the fields,' said de Roemer. 'They may be worth thousands of Lats, but they have to work.'

Beyond the course, sledges waiting for the next race paraded round and round on the level surface of the lake, the horses breaking into a trot from time to time to shake off the cold. A race was in progress, the sledges rounding the far bend of the course. The favourite, a gipsy dressed in a tight-waisted mustard yellow sheepskin, suddenly ran into the bank, over-turned his sledge and fell out. He was up again in a moment and finished second, but he was greeted by a shower of curses from his backers and in a moment the whole group was embroiled in a savage fight.

By now, it was one o'clock and de Roemer suggested that we should go out into the country and visit some peasants he knew. 'We won't stop to eat. I've got something here.' He pulled the bread from his pocket and turned for our assent, the inevitable '*Qui Papa*' of the children being taken for granted.

'I think we had better have some soup,' I ventured, and so we went into a small restaurant, warm at least, but reeking intoler-ably of boiled cabbage and stale food.

'The proprietress is a very nice woman, the widow of a Polish officer,' said de Roemer.

A tired-looking woman brought a large bowl of broth and some hot *piroshki*. The children ate hungrily, being allowed to finish the vegetables that lay in the bottom of the bowl.

When we reached the peasants' house a savage dog sprang at the horses and held them at bay, its teeth bared. At last de

Roemer, having cowed the dog by threatening it with a stone, tramped through the snow and knocked on the door. Two minutes later we were warming ourselves at a huge stove. The walls were hung with musical instruments made by hand, even to the screws, by the sons of the house. A loom filled nearly a quarter of the room. The old woman opened a chest and lifted out stuffs home-dyed and hand-woven from the wool of her own sheep.

Presently the peasant came in, his little eyes twinkling with pleasure at the sight of de Roemer. Then standing with his back to the stove he launched into an endless lament.

'He's telling the story of the horse they lost last autumn,' explained Christophe. 'For them it's almost as bad as losing a child.'

When we returned to Rezekne, de Roemer at last suggested eating. The widow of the Polish officer, now wearing a Sunday dress trimmed with greasy frills, offered us fish or pork. The tablecloth was stained with food which had slopped over from well-filled plates. In the poorer parts of the world one so often finds small plates piled high to suggest abundance. For me, to swallow each mouthful was a discipline, but there was no escape since stale cooking smells and soiled linen were everywhere, and food was too precious to be slighted.

When we reached the train we uncorked yesterday's bottle of soda water, crushed an aspirin each and swallowed it. Then, lying at full length on the wooden seat, my head on Kenneth's knees, I let the hours pass, dimly conscious of movement and noise, and the jar as the train stopped and started.

Gradually the images of the day returned—Jola quietly submissive to an iron discipline; Christophe absorbed in the delicate work of his long thin fingers; de Roemer, a stone figure carved on a tomb with five diminutive obedient stone children kneeling at his feet. Catholic Belgium, Poland and the Teutonic Knights; cold, hunger and weariness.

'I am a soldier of the church militant,' he said. 'What is the flesh but weakness.'

CHAPTER 14

In the grip of the bitter winter of '39 to '40, man-made misery was extending in all directions. Germany decided to consolidate its hold on the more prosperous western areas of Poland and decreed mass transportations of peasants to the lands bordering the new Russian frontier. Their holdings were to be taken over by peasants from Bavaria and Silesia.

In Finland, disregarding President Kallio's appeal for an honourable peace, the Russians launched a massive attack on the Mannerheim Line. The Siberian ski battalion was wiped out and the 34th Moscow Tank Brigade annihilated in the fight for Viipuri, but Russian reserves were inexhaustible.

Britain and France offered war materials to Finland, but with German vessels now patrolling the coasts of Denmark and Norway, delivery was not easy. Twenty-eight thousand Danish families offered homes to refugee children and Swedish municipalities adopted neighbouring Finnish towns, sending administrators to replace the men who had gone to war. But all the goodwill, and desperate bravery of the Finns were of no avail against the overwhelming weight of the Russian attack, and on March 12th Finland was obliged to capitulate, yielding to Russia the defences of the Mannerheim Line, the Karelian Isthmus and

Viipuri, the fortified town on the coast between Leningrad and Helsinki. The Russians returned the port of Petsamo on the Arctic Circle to the Finns, but claimed right of passage through it to Norway and put a limit on the number of vessels the Finns could keep there. A special railway was to be built along the shortest route from Russia to Sweden, over which the Russians claimed right of way.

The Finns, with one-eighth of their population already homeless, were to re-house 400,000 people, mainly refugees from the lost lands of Karelia which had provided one tenth of Finland's arable land. It was a bitter harvest from an unprovoked war.

Meanwhile, although Roosevelt declared that the 'moral embargo' against Russia was still in force, it was clear to Italy that strong-arm tactics paid off, and Mussolini and Hitler met on the Brenner to discuss future collaboration.

The United Kingdom had so far suffered nothing more serious than the bombs planted by the IRA. In early February five IRA members who had been responsible for the deaths of five people and the wounding of a hundred more in Coventry the previous September, were condemned to death at the Old Bailey.

In Riga, the snow continued to fall and finally defeated the efforts of the municipal cleaners to clear it away. The problem was temporarily solved by pushing the surplus snow into a ridge down the middle of the road, creating a miniature two-lane highway. Notices were posted everywhere warning people to keep their distance from the houses as great masses of snow frequently slid down, jumping the snow-guards and landing on the pavement with a thumping flurry.

During the previous summer the Latvians had made a film called 'The Fisherman's Son' which was now on show, and so popular that one had to book days in advance. The story, which

Lotte explained to us, was simple but the photographs of the beach and forest and the river mouth near our dacha were hauntingly beautiful. On the first night the people showed their appreciation by forcing and breaking the glass doors of the cinema, and the police reported finding seventeen goloshes and fifty-eight buttons when the crowd had dispersed.

As the ice sealed the Baltic to shipping and the crippling cold interrupted air line schedules, diplomatic Bags became rarer and the intervals between letters from home longer and more nerve-wracking. The search for alternative routes for mail became an obsession. A notice appeared in the Riga Post Office that letters to England would travel via Poland and Romania. This had probably been printed before the collapse of Poland, and was quickly taken down. Rumour had it that letters addressed to neutral countries would go in sealed mail bags through Germany so we decided to write to a Swiss friend living in Davos and ask if she would forward letters to England and vice versa. She agreed warmly, but only one letter came through. The rest, having made the double journey through Germany, were returned marked 'No Postal Communication'.

The next attempt followed a notice in *Briva Zeme* that an air mail would leave Moscow for England on the 10th and 25th of each month. This proved tantamount to dropping the mail into an oubliette and might even have been a clumsy device for keeping the Russian censorship department occupied. A letter from my mother, which had taken nearly five weeks on the way, reached us bearing British, German and Finnish censorship labels. Our experiments came to an end when, after the German invasion of Norway and Denmark, the Riga Post Office announced that no more mail would be accepted for England.

From time to time the Bag brought precious letters from my mother and the boys. Though happy at school, they obviously felt the loss of their home in Riga and were wistful about the things they had been obliged to leave behind. Sam was particularly concerned about the wooden boat he had made. 'If you will send it,' he wrote, 'I will pay the postage as long as it is not above 1/-, which it should not be. It is old, and it is war, so I don't see why I should pay much customs.' We explained the postal difficulties and said we would do our best. The letter postage rate in England had just risen to 2 1/2 d and Sam wrote that he had sent a letter to himself to commemorate the event.

Earlier in the winter the Latvian Government had organized an expedition to Sigulda for which the Diplomatic Corps were expected to dress up in ski clothes and proceed over the snow to a grandstand which gave a good view of one of the rare ski jumps in the country. After some hasty coaching our own Minister was still uncertain on skis. Each time he fell, he was courteously helped to his feet by the German Minister, perhaps out of kindness or possibly because he was blocking the *piste.* In spite of plentiful vodka and the Latvian *Glühwein* made from brown bread and apples, the presence of so many elderly diplomats and the high standard of politeness made the going a little slow, so we decided with our French colleagues that we would organize a more adventurous outing. Having arranged a Saturday morning off, we set out by train the previous evening. There were seven of us in the party, de Beausse the French First Secretary and their Commercial Attaché Malgrat, our own Military Attaché Croxton Vale, Tom Brimelow and a Latvian guide.

As usual the train dawdled along with frequent stops for refuelling.

'You know why they run the trains so slow,' Malgrat observed. 'It's to make the country seem bigger. *C'est malin.*'

To enjoy this decelerated travel one would have to adopt the mentality of the peasants, who believe that to travel is more interesting than to arrive, and are prepared to settle down at a station indefinitely like seals on a beach, indifferent to cold draughts and hard floors.

At Madona sledges were waiting and we piled in, I in the first with Croxton and a Polish driver. The other three sledges followed, one with a local driver and the other two driven by the guide, Kenneth and de Beausse in turn.

In Latvia, transport often follows a different course in winter, crossing lakes and swamps which would be impass-able during the summer months. After a heavy fall of snow the track becomes invisible and the horse is left to find its own way without interference from the driver. Many a peasant has been brought home dead from exposure after a drunken bout, the beast being unaware that anything was amiss with its master.

Stars shimmered above a light mist which shone whitely with the reflection of the snow. The horses trudged on through an immense silence. Not a light could be seen. The rare farmhouse was shuttered and black. Occasionally someone called '*nu, nu*' to a horse. The other two sledges plodded quietly after us, mile after mile.

From time to time the silence would be broken with cries of 't-r-r-r' to bring the sledges to a halt. One of the horses had missed the track and plunged into the deep snow, capsizing its sledge and temporarily burying the occupants.

About two in the morning, chilled and drowsy, we reached a farmhouse and were welcomed by the peasants with hot milk and home-baked bread spread with honey and wild strawberry jam. The farmer's wife showed us into two dormitories with eight narrow beds in one and three in the other. The smaller one was allotted to Kenneth and me. In the centre of the floor stood the white chamber pot which was always offered to the ladies of a party on arrival at a farmhouse.

While we were tugging off our boots the others came into our room to discuss arrangements for the next day, all but de Beausse, whom we could see through the open door kneeling at his bed in prayer. De Beausse, a devout Catholic and father of eight children, was one of the small group of aristocrats one used to meet in the French Foreign Service who continued to work in an increasingly distasteful *ambience* from a strong sense of duty.

As we went into the kitchen for breakfast next morning Malgrat came in from the garden shouting with laughter. 'Venez, venez voir le petit Monr Blanc.'

One by one we were conducted to the outside privy. From the centre of the hole cut in the wooden bench rose a small symmetrical peak—more like Fujiyama than Mont Blanc in fact—capped with a neat topping of snow which had blown in during the night. Normally the ample depths of a Latvian privy can cope discreetly with the accumulations of a whole winter, which remain perfectly inoffensive at low temperatures, but the abnormal cold had deep-frozen deposits as they touched down and produced this towering oddity.

The sun was shining brilliantly as we set out for Mount Gaisina, the goal of our expedition. One thousand and twenty-three feet above sea level, though only a few hundred feet higher than the surrounding country, this was an object of pride to the Latvians. For us, it was a relief to enjoy a few minutes of down-hill run after the usual hours of *langlauf*.

Lunch at the farmhouse was excellent, with thick peasant soup and roast veal. The thoughtful French had provided two tins of the Ambassador's precious sardines and several bottles of Burgundy. That evening we ate only bread and butter, enlivened by a couple of bottles of champagne contributed by the British, and awarded to the man who had made the most spectacular tumbles during the day.

Next morning, our rucksacks were piled into the sledges and we set out for a run of thirty kilometres over deep snow with a frozen crust which continually broke to trap one's skis. A farmhouse lunch of turkey soup, roast pork with cabbage, followed by stewed apples and bilberries piled with whipped cream raised our spirits temporarily. This time we drank claret. As darkness fell our guide lost his way and we limped over the final kilometre only just in time to catch the last train of the day.

As the situation in Europe deteriorated the number of visa applicants, with or without hope, increased. Ciphering was a continual burden both in and out of office hours. Besides this, it was decided that a useful source of semi-overt intelligence on trends and conditions in the Soviet Union should come to the office twice a week during the afternoon. This man, always referred to as 'Our Friend', had the sharp features and rufous colouring of a dog fox, accentuated by the tawny fur collar which muffled his cheeks and mingled with the fur of his *papacha*.

His arrival, by way of the mews at the back of the building, was heralded by three little rings at the door of the former servants' entrance, which was opened by Dorothy Corrie after a careful peep through the 'magic eye' fixed in the centre panel.

Dorothy then returned to her work and Our Friend would settle on the one empty chair in my cubby hole and, unfolding copy after copy of *Pravda* and *Izvestia* would read aloud the interesting pieces, translating them into German as he went along. These I took down on my typewriter in English. Sometimes a request would come from Head Office to pay particular attention to reports on a certain factory, or signs that supplies of such and such a product were breaking down. Some of the most interesting articles were the obligatory pieces of self-criticism, when the manager of a big industrial combine or a state production unit would be selected to confess that output had fallen by X number of tons; that so and so many workers had been sent for corrective detention in Siberia; that the whole production of tractors from a certain works had proved unfit for use. To a Westerner, such outpourings would appear a poor advertisement for the Soviet system, and hardly calculated to encourage Russia's ally, Germany, but unless they had served the Government's purpose, they would certainly not have appeared.

One morning in early April we saw the first blades of grass for nearly four months, in a sheltered patch on the south-facing bank of the canal. They were not a fresh green promise of spring, however, but brown and crushed and rather a reminder of the iron repression of winter.

People were still crossing the frozen Daugave on foot, though spreading pools of melt-water made the operation look increasingly unsafe. This rather risky short-cut came to an abrupt end when news arrived that broken ice, coming down the river from Russia, was piling up to threaten the power station at Kegums and must be allowed free passage to the sea. The ice below the Riga bridges had to be dynamited immediately.

Crowds gathered on the ice just upstream of where the charges were being laid and watched with apparent unconcern as the explosions cut a clean line from bank to bank and the broken ice floated downstream to leave open water only a few yards from the line of spectators.

Before the ice had ceased to threaten the power station Norway and Denmark were invaded by the Germans, and Miggs, in Stockholm, was now like us cut off by land and sea.

With a thaw in sight, passengers on the ski trains were now regularly conscripted for an hour or two to load onto carts the logs stacked by the railway tracks, as once warmer weather set in all the horses would be needed for ploughing, sowing and harvesting and there was not sufficient motor transport to distribute the stocks of wood. The thaw would also mean a temporary shortage of fresh fish. In winter these could be caught through holes in the ice to which the fish flocked, attracted by the light, sometimes in such numbers that they could be scooped out in bucketfuls. Normal fishing could not be resumed until the ice had melted.

On Sunday April 7th we decided to take a last look at the frozen sea and walked along the beach at Bulduri. The ice, wrought into strange textures by the action of the waves, stretched to the horizon. We walked out over the sea for about half a mile but still there was no sign of open water. Just ahead lay a sheet of diamonds, glittering in the sun. Coming nearer, we saw that some reaction of thaw and frost had formed crystal feathers, each about ten inches long and standing upright on the ice bed. Every plume was delicately fretted and swayed in the breeze, curving at the tip and catching the sunlight with a blinding flash. It was like the ruffled breast of a gigantic silver goose.

Further out, the ice had piled up in huge blocks, forming mounds thirty feet high. Some great chunks stood on one edge, appearing precariously balanced, but in reality immovable. It was difficult to guess what force had thrown up these monstrous lumps, since the ice stretched smoothly seawards without any sign of violence caused by a storm. A few days later all these marvels had vanished without trace, leaving open sea.

Spring came overnight and with it a longing for the fresh air of the beach and forest. Dick and Kathleen Whishaw, who both came of Anglo-Russian families, had a dacha by the Lielupe. In the garden was a small detached house. There was one room downstairs and, reached by an outside stair, two small bedrooms and what the Germans so compactly describe as a *Waschgelegenheit* or means of washing—in this case a cold tap and a china basin—perfectly adequate with a beach of white sand and the clear water of the river just at the bottom of the garden. The loo was hidden behind a clump of sunflowers.

'The children used the small *dacha* for their friends,' said Kathleen Whishaw. 'You need bring nothing from Riga but your swimming things and anything Lotte needs. She can share our kitchen and sleep with our cook. We should love to have you.'

The offer was too good to miss, even if half our nights would have to be spent on cipher standby in Riga. Lotte was delighted.

'Vufi will guard the small *dacha* when you are away. Once a week I shall go to Riga and clean the flat and do the washing,' she assured me, 'and see that there is everything you need when you are there.'

On our first night at the *dacha* a soft spring rain was falling, fresh with the scent of pines and moss. Buds were unfolding so fast in the early warmth that one would return in the evening to find a tree transformed. Humans eagerly adopted the joyful domesticity of the small animals and birds, all sensing the urgency of the short-lived summer.

Two days later, on May 10th, the Germans without warning invaded France, Holland, Belgium and Luxembourg. The serious war in Europe had began.

Rotterdam fell and the Dutch Royal Family and the Netherlands Government arrived in London. A Bag from Stockholm brought a letter from Miggs saying that should the Germans invade Sweden she was to join a small mobile party which would accompany the Swedish Government in flight up country. On May 30th the British army was cornered at Dunkirk and during the next four days the historic rescue operation across the Channel took place. Churchill made his famous speech, '... we shall fight them on the beaches, we shall fight them on the landing grounds, we shall fight them in the fields and in the streets, we shall fight them in the hills; we shall never surrender.'

A letter from my mother dated June 4th declared, 'Britain must win. Never doubt it.'

Seen from a distance and with evidence of the crushing force of the enemy so near to us, this seemed a pathetic, though admirable, delusion. This feeling was clearly shared by the Germans who were now much in evidence in Riga. By agreement with the Latvian Government, two thousand of the Balts who had assumed German nationality were allowed to remain in Riga to liquidate the assets of the evacuees. These were all hardcore Nazis, regarded by the German Government as reliable.

The commuter train to the Strand and lunch at our usual restaurant had now become an ordeal, as copies of the *Berliner Tageblatt* were spread wide while one well-fed German called to another details of the latest military success.

In contrast, the German Minister, a diplomat of the old school, politely agreed to please his Latvian hosts at the Tennis Club party by leading the Lambeth Walk. This was excused by his staff as being really a piece of anti-British propaganda, since the song recalled the suffering of prisoners forced in olden times to cross the Thames at low tide, and throwing their manacled hands in the air as they cried out in fear of drowning.

While we were tied more closely than ever to the office, Lotte was enjoying the *dacha,* especially since the change of air was doing her plants good. The date palm which should have sheltered her in her old age had come to a premature end, since she had tried to reproduce its native climate by standing it in the oven. Its place had been taken by another sprouting date stone, a relic of Christmas dinner, which at present showed only a spike the size of a gramophone needle. Her prize exhibit was a mysterious plant that had developed three leaves with the texture of green linoleum, and an enigmatic knob of the same appearance.

June 15th was to be Mark's eleventh birthday and he had written to ask for details of the one he had spent in Rindseln six years before, as he was busy writing the story of his life. Anukelchen, we told him, had dressed both boys in skirts of mare's tails and made them crowns of flowers. A throne covered in lilac had been arranged for Mark on the verandah and beside it a birthday table with four candles and a *Kringel* topped with shiny walnuts and caramelized sugar. His special present was a small yellow cart with blue wheels and we took it in turns to pull him up and down under the chestnut trees until he was daring enough to career down the slope from the great house on his own. The yellow cart was still in the loft when we had last visited Rindseln.

This year, on Mark's birthday, following an ultimatum handed to the government by Molotov, Russian troops marched into Lithuania. Molotov accused the Lithuanians of kidnapping Soviet soldiers, with the connivance of local officials, and demanded the trial of General Skucas, Minister of the Interior and Chief of the Political Police. Paleckis, a collaborator with the Russians, was entrusted with the formation of the Lithuanian 'people's government' friendly to the USSR.

CHAPTER 15

On June 17th there was thunder in the air and everyone's nerves were on edge. Communications with the outside world were cut, and there was a general feeling of uneasiness. As we returned to the office after lunch we heard a distant rumbling. People were hurrying, like leaves before the wind, down the broad Brivibas iela towards the centre of the town. As we crossed the corner of the Raina Boulevard the first Russian tanks came in sight.

There was no time to be lost. We must start burning our confidential documents at once. Within a few minutes black smoke was rising from the chimneys of all the Legations.

Nothing is more frustrating than burning paper in a hurry. Separated sheet by sheet it flares up dangerously and takes an age to get through a pile, but if you put a solid block of paper into the fire it remains as serenely unscathed as Shadrach, Meshak and Abednigo.

For the next few hours all four of us knelt, each in front of a tall Russian stove, and fed through the small door the confidential work of years. The naked flames were confined to the single opening, but as the afternoon wore on the great porcelain flanks, running from floor to ceiling, became too hot to touch. To avoid congestion, ash had be to raked out frequently, and settled on our hair and skin, making our eyes smart. Our faces became painfully scorched, until we hit on the idea of shielding them with a mask made of cardboard with slits for the eyes.

Each knock on the door or footfall in the outer office made our hearts thump painfully. From time to time Dorothy brewed a great pot of tea which almost hissed as it went down.

Towards seven o'clock, grimy and exhausted, we could rest at last. The outer office with its visa records presented an appearance of solid bona fides. Stationery cupboards and shelves of reference books stood neatly in the private offices, but the filing cabinets were empty.

This had been a very different experience from the days spent clearing the Legation in Vienna before it was taken over by the Luftwaffe, who had bought it from the British Government. There were no stoves in the building and the boiler in the basement normally used for destroying confidential waste had proved quite inadequate for dealing with papers going back to the '80s, so we had dragged the garden incinerator beneath the window of my office and stirred the burning paper with a long pole while we dangled our legs in the spring sunshine as we sat on the sill. From time to time the Austrian Gestapo, who had moved into the building which formed the other side of the courtyard, amused themselves by leaning out of the windows and trying to snatch the charred papers as they floated up in a sudden breeze. When I tried to catch up on my press reading they followed my eyes backwards and forwards across the newspaper with the reflected light from a pocket mirror.

Out in the streets of Riga the ordinary citizens hurried by apprehensively as crowds of rough-looking people swarmed into the centre of town. The Communist Party, being illegal, had gone underground, but now it was emerging with its banners and slogans from the industrial suburbs across the river.

At the sight of a Russian tank, placed strategically to enfilade the pontoon bridge, the workers stopped and raised a loud cheer for the Red Army and their Communist comrades. Suddenly the hatch on top of the tank opened and a Russian soldier, dusty and drawn-looking, like the rest of the troops who had made the long haul from the frontier, climbed out. Quite deliberately he strode towards the cheer leader and knocked him down. 'Shut your flaming traps,' he shouted menacingly. 'We want to get some sleep.'

The unconscious workman was dragged aside and those behind, who had not seen the incident, pressed on, well satisfied with their first contact with the Red Army.

As we approached the Town Hall Square the mood of the crowd was ugly. Men were prising up paving stones and throwing them at the police, two of whom stood at the corner, back to back, their faces grey, their revolvers swinging in a slow arc in an attempt to intimidate the crowd. But those behind pushed others forward and with the square jammed with people the policemen's chances looked slim.

At this moment a Russian tank rumbled up the street. A machine gun was mounted on the roof.

As late comers we were at the back of the crowd, but being eager to see what was happening, we managed to clamber onto the steps of a building bordering the square, remembering guiltily my father's warning that it was the curious outsider who caught the stray bullet.

A soldier emerged from the turret of the tank and motioned to the policemen to step back. There was a moment's hush, and then someone waved a red flag and the masses surged forward once more. With an angry rattle the gunner swung his weapon, sending a swathe of bullets into the densely-packed crowd. There was a moment of total silence and then screams as the onlookers struggled to push past the dead and dying and escape. The soldier watched dispassionately, his hand on the trigger. Within moments the square was empty but for the bodies on the ground, some still, some writhing. The policemen slipped their revolvers into the holsters. The turret of the tank closed as it drew off, and we hurried through the gathering dusk in the direction of home. As we reached our part of the town not a soul was to be seen on the streets.

'I think the local Communists are in for a surprise,' said Kenneth. 'The Russian army isn't going to stand disorder here any more than it would at home.'

Next morning the newspapers informed the people of Latvia and Estonia that since their governments had failed to annul their pacts of mutual assistance, and had even sought to extend them to include Lithuania and Finland, they had violated the agreements each had signed with the Soviet Union in 1931. The USSR therefore demanded a change of government in both countries and unlimited entry for their troops.

As we walked to the office next morning we saw that the Russians had roped off the vast Esplanade and turned it into a military camp with field kitchens and improvised washing arrangements round the hydrants. Rows of tanks and lorries were drawn up on the perimeter. All round the square people crowded to the ropes, watching the scene like visitors to a zoo. Although the men had apparently slept on the ground, most of them had washed off the white dust of the journey and brushed their uniforms.

Each important crossroads in the town was commanded by a Russian tank and all buildings of importance were guarded by Russian sentries. Here and there a flag hung limply, but the streets were quiet. Not so our office, which spilled a queue of terrified applicants right through the Consulate and out onto the path. Stories of Russian anti-semitism had reached Riga.

We hoped for some message from the Director of Latvian Army Intelligence, hitherto a useful source of information, but in vain. On the previous day his chimneys, like ours, had belched the telltale black smoke.

During the morning the Latvian radio announced that President Ulmanis urged his countrymen to go about their business as usual, though no one knew how long he would be able to follow his own excellent advice. The papers headlined the news that Andrei Vyshinsky, the Soviet Deputy Foreign Minister, would be arriving in Riga next morning and would make a speech from the balcony of the Soviet Legation in the afternoon. As Chief Prosecutor during the 1936–8 show trials of the old Party members and Soviet Generals, Vyshinsky had called for such savage sentences that he became known as 'the butcher'.

The Latvian State Optical Works had recently produced the first of the miniature cameras, the Minox, which was being eagerly bought by representatives of all the foreign intelligence services in Riga, and is now being manufactured in the West. At London's request we had sent a number of these home through the Bag for clandestine use, but we had not yet tested one. Here was an opportunity to tryout their efficacy in the field. It was decided that Glyn Hall, with his fluent Russian and untidy, bucolic appearance, would be the right person for the experiment. As a further qualification, he had no diplomatic status so, should there be trouble, the Legation could disclaim responsibility. I was to accompany him and add an air of casual sightseeing to our slightly perilous outing.

With the help of Dorothy Corrie, Glyn fixed the Minox, which was little bigger than a Dunhill lighter, beneath the lapel of his jacket and I put on an old straw hat which might prove handy cover if we wished to change a film.

A procession was streaming up the Elizabetes iela escorted by tanks decked with flowers. We soon found ourselves jammed in the crowd, all looking up expectantly at the flag-draped balcony where Vychinsky was to appear. As at all recent demonstrations the crowd was a rough one but, with Russian soldiers posted at frequent intervals along the route and tanks in the background, likely to be well behaved.

Suddenly my hat was snatched from my head. I whipped round in alarm, but it was only an old peasant woman. 'Better not wear a hat, my dear,' she cautioned. 'These Russians are not used to ladies and gentlemen.'

Vyshinsky, a grey-haired man looking more like a bureau-crat than a butcher, acknowledged the cheers of the crowd and launched into a long speech, made even longer by regular pauses for applause. Over and over again he repeated 'Za mir, za hleb, za svobodu naroda'—'Peace, bread and a free people'—the old battle cry of the Bolsheviks. To a popula-tion which, for the past twenty years, had enjoyed peace and a high standard of living, and free-est period of their whole history, this slogan, had they stopped to think, did not offer any unaccustomed benefits. It was even doubtful whether a large proportion of the crowd could hear what Vychinsky was saying, but this was a day off—with the factories closed and the sun shining.

There had been only one hundred and fifty registered members of the underground Communist Party in Latvia but as always, for every declared Communist there were scores of fellow travellers and hundreds ready to jump on the band waggon.

Gradually we worked our way nearer the balcony. Furtively Glynn pressed the button on the little Minox. The scenes we were snapping would appear in the morning papers and the

Russians should have no objection to their wider distribution. What we were trying to show, and what the Russians would certainly not approve, was that one could take adequate pictures of a given scene without being noticed.

As the afternoon wore on and the enthusiasm of the crowd seemed inexhaustible, Vyshinsky gave up any effort to hand out the party line and shouted 'Latvia, Latvia'. This went down well, but so did 'Pretty girls', 'Happy days', and various other encouraging inanities which he called out from time to time. Finally, to our astonishment, Vyshinsky and the Soviet Minister were doing a sort of double turn, addressing the crowd as 'Latvian citizens' and referring to the 'independence of Latvia'. We could only think that lunch at the Soviet Legation must have been exceptionally good.

When Vyshinsky's performance came to an end the crowd moved off to the Ministry of War. Finding it heavily guarded, they surged on to the President's palace and started to break the windows, demanding that the Red Flag be hoisted from the Castle Tower. However, hearing the rumble of tanks the crowd quickly dispersed.

'We don't have hooligans like that in Russia,' one soldier remarked. 'Hooligan' had in fact become a popular Russian term of censure and when Phyllis MacKillop had tried to push her way onto a crowded tram in Moscow she was reproved by a would-be passenger for being a 'guliganka'.

Having dealt with the public relations side of his visit, Vyshinsky proceeded to dismiss President Ulmanis and all his ministers and set up a provisional administration, the purpose of which was to hold elections which would result in a Communist government. The date of the elections was fixed for July 14th.

Meanwhile, in a few days the aspect of Riga was completely altered without any revolutionary changes having been carried out. The transformation was insidious, like the deterioration caused by a flock of chickens let loose in an orchard. Pavements were no longer swept and litter, fortunately rare in Latvia, lay where it fell. The old women disappeared from the parks and the flowers faded on their stalks in this hot June.

Police had vanished from the streets, their place being taken by soldiers directing the traffic with small improvised red flags. Illuminated signs, advertisements for a capitalist economy, were turned off and had not yet been replaced by the giant red stars so beloved of the Russian administration. Shop windows, nearly empty now, were unlit. People who normally dressed smartly now wore their oldest clothes and there was a pervading drabness, and an almost tangible depression. Those who were not afraid of the future in a People's Socialist Republic were nevertheless disappointed at the repressive discipline that they met at almost every turn.

The Russians, in fact, were facing an awkward problem. Ever since the Revolution there had been an acute shortage of consumer goods in Soviet Russia and, as even today, dwelling space was strictly limited. The evidence of Latvian prosperity could not be eliminated overnight, but in the meantime the armed forces must be given some explanation why a small country under a 'corrupt capitalist administration' could achieve for its people a standard of living so much higher than in Russia.

The story was put about, and apparently believed by the more naive members of the occupying forces, that Riga was part of a great exhibition and that the city would shortly return to normal.

CHAPTER 16

With the office work-load increasing every day and the situation so uncertain it was only possible to snatch an occasional night at the *dacha,* so Lotte returned to Riga, with her plants and Vufi crammed into an oilcloth bag.

The moments of escape to the Strand were wonderfully peaceful and restoring. The train service had been severely reduced and the carriages were now crowded and no longer clean, so on arrival at the *dacha* we plunged into the river. After this, the men would chop wood for the kitchen stove or tackle some project in Dick's workshop, while Kathleen and I chatted as she watered the rings of pansies round the fruit trees and the bright petunias she had planted in the window boxes of our small house.

Kathleen's family had lived for generations in St Petersburg and when young, she and her sister were known as the 'beautiful Misses Gellibrand'. Dick, too, came from an Anglo-Russian family and he would amuse us with stories of his boyhood and how, when he was sent to boarding school in England, the boys insisted on calling him 'Jomskikoff', and asking why there was no snow on his boots.

After supper, as the light slowly faded, we would watch the

132

rafts of pine logs drifting down the river, tied together to form a snake sometimes as much as half a kilometre long, guided round the bends by men with poles who jumped from one raft to another. Along the arc of the bridge navigation lights flashed as the sun dipped towards midnight, green for the boat channel and a red warning when the centre span swung out to allow the passage of a steamer.

With the escape route to the UK virtually cut, the demand for British visas had eased but now, in spite of the threat of Arab violence, the unfortunate Jews were determined to use any means of getting to Palestine. Though the main immigration quota was full for months to come, there was one visa category still open to a number of people in Riga. Anyone who could prove that he owned £1,000 worth of property in Palestine, or a like sum deposited in a bank there, could have a so-called capitalist visa. This was meant to ensure that such immigrants would not become a charge on the limited resources of the territory then under British mandate.

Most of the people with 'capitalist' qualifications had hitherto been comfortably established in Riga and unwilling to abandon their homes and businesses. Now, however, anything seemed better than to fall a victim to Russian anti-semitism, and applications for capitalist visas came flooding in. According to the rules such applications had to be sent to London and then forwarded to Palestine for authentification of the claims. If the reply was favourable, London authorized the visa. Even in peace time this procedure was slow but now, with communications disrupted, it was proving of little practical use. So we hit on a scheme by which we would send a reply-paid telegram to Barclay's Bank in Tel Aviv or Haifa, briefly worded, for example 'Abraham Heimann, 56 Hayarkon Street, Tel Aviv' or 'Israel Blaufeld, £1,500, Bank of the Middle East, Haifa'. Barclay's would then check the ownership of the property or sum mentioned and wire back 'Correct'—or sometimes not. Applicants were asked to deposit the approximate cost of the telegram and collect the change when the reply came in. In this way a visa for Palestine could be granted in a few days and perhaps a whole family saved. Customs and passport controls were still maintained at the former Russian frontier, and visas were required by Latvians to pass this point, but the Russians were happy to give transit visas for the long rail journey to the Black Sea and rid themselves of what they regarded as undesirable elements who would conveniently leave their wealth behind.

The Jewish Agency and our contact there, Herr Schonberg, a kindly white-haired patriarch, worked indefatigably for these unhappy victims of so many political cross-currents. As we gained his confidence he would accept our assurance that everything possible had been done in a given case, and we gradually came to depend on him to give an honest assessment of the bona fides of an applicant.

At the end of June the police were beginning to reappear in the streets of Riga. Russian officers, meticulously saluted by their men, walked about sedately in pairs like children who have had too strict a governess. Other ranks were beginning to fraternize with Latvian girls, though some were intimidated by their very simple make-up. 'They are so painted they make our tanks shy,' said one soldier. When not on duty the troops preferred to loll comfortably, relaxing quite happily on the tarpaulin covering their lorry, unlike the German troops in Vienna, who seemed unable to shed their military personalities.

As we were waiting to cross the Brivibas iela a lorry stopped beside us and a pedestrian ventured a little cautious teasing. 'Can you get clothes in Russia?' he called to the men on the truck. 'As much as you like,' one of them answered. 'What about boots?' 'We have all the boots you want in Russia.' 'Then why didn't you stay there?' The only answer was a grin.

The Russian-language newspaper *Sevodnia* had been replaced by the *Russkaya Gazeta* and Russian news films were now shown instead of Latvian. The National War Memorial, which commemorated *inter alia* the liberation of Latvia from the Russian invaders at the end of the First World War, was however heaped each day with fresh flowers. The sale of vodka was still banned, but the waiter at our usual lunchtime restaurant asked to our surprise if we would like water with our zakouski. 'A little water does you good,' he remarked, giving us each a small tumbler. (Vodka is the diminutive of *voda,* the Russian word for water.)

'Just like the old dry days back home,' commented Reinhardt, the American Vice-Consul who often lunched with us.

On July 4th the British navy sank the French battleships in Oran harbour as they were leaving Algeria to join Admiral Darlan's collaborationist fleet, and Petain broke off diplomatic relations with Great Britain. Now we should be deprived of contact with our French colleagues.

News came that our Minister, Charles Orde, was transferred to Chile, and on the eighth we saw him off at the Moscow Station on the long route via Siberia, Dairen and the Pacific, having fulfilled our promise to Mrs Orde and collected all the small comforts we could find for his journey.

Taking advantage of the night-long twilight of high summer to make a useful economy, the Russians had turned off the street lighting. Beneath the trees of the boulevards people moved, mysteriously quiet, in the rich soft dusk. But when the elections were only a week away, the lights were switched on again to give clear vision in case there should be the need to shoot. Everyone was perfectly free to vote as he pleased—for the single

Communist list—but not to abstain, as an identity card without a stamp from the polling booth could lead to very serious trouble. Using the same methods as his Nazi allies, Stalin felt confident of a 98% majority.

In order that the workers should not be needlessly absent from their jobs a public holiday had been chosen for election day. Normally this would have been a Sunday, but Sundays had been abolished, their place being taken by one day off in six, an improvement, as the radio pointed out, on the Almighty's one day in seven.

Before the Russians could get down to the real business of taking over the country foreign witnesses must be removed, so the new government announced that as Latvia wished to form part of the Union of Soviet Socialist Republics it would no longer require independent diplomatic relations, and all associated privileges would be withdrawn on August 1st. In other words, foreign diplomats who stayed on after the deadline would be without protection. This information was passed on to London and we waited confidently for instructions to leave.

With only a fortnight to go before the expiry date the furniture vans were busy once more as the Legations packed up for their return home. Harold Hobson had already left to be Consul in Havana. MacKillop had gone to Stockholm, and still there was no word about our future movements. With the Germans occupying the whole of North-west Europe, and Italy and France blocking the Mediterranean, our choice of escape routes was narrowing. We could go to Stockholm or Helsinki but would have to remain, as did Miggs in Sweden, for the rest of the war, and both Legations were already fully staffed.

If we were to return home our choice lay between two long and circuitous routes. The first was through Moscow, Odessa and thence in a series of hops to Damascus, Basra, Bombay,

Durban and home round the Cape. The second was by the Trans-Siberian Railway through Manchukuo, Dairen, Japan and Canada. Each would require a variety of transit visas so, with the Legations closing all round us, we decided to ignore the lack of orders from home and collect every visa we could possibly use.

Our opposite numbers were extremely helpful, sometimes digging deep into crates for the visa stamps which had already been packed—all but the French, whose visa staff appeared to be Petainistes to a man. Very unwillingly they consented to stamp in our passports the Syrian visas which would allow us to pass through Damascus.

'What do we owe?' I asked.

'Unfortunately we cannot make a charge,' replied the official ungraciously. I pushed four full fees into the *Croix Rouge* box still standing on the counter. As we were leaving the office one of the doors in the passage opened a crack and Malgrat's face appeared.

'The de Roemer boy was seen in a ditch on the retreat to Bordeaux,' he whispered. 'He had been cycling along beside the troops and his bicycle was damaged, the front wheel I think. I thought you'd like to know.'

'Have you heard nothing more?' I asked. He shook his head and the door closed softly.

Greatly relieved to have acquired all the visas we might need, including the American and the Japanese, we telegraphed to London asking them to reply with the single words 'Trans-Siberian' or 'the Cape'.

Unaware of the true reasons for the restraint shown so far by the Russians, the man in the street had come to think that his apprehensions might have been exaggerated. The correct behaviour of the Red Army and the friendliness of the soldiers had furthered this impression. With the eager blindness of wishful thinking the simpler people had persuaded themselves that life under the Russians would be quite tolerable. Those who thought differently wisely refrained from airing their views. The newspapers described the marvels of the Soviet Union, which stretched from Germany to Japan; sheep with wool down to their ankles in Azerbaijan, grapes like drops of blood in the Caucasus; perpetual summer on the Black Sea, millions of silk worms in Daghestan.

On July 21st the puppet governments of the three Baltic States applied to join the Soviet Union.

On the same day, in all three States, land was nationalized and farmers learnt to their dismay that each would be allowed the use of a maximum of thirty acres—a completely unviable unit. This land, which now belonged to the State, could not be bought or sold. The nationalization was described as a measure to end the sufferings of the peasantry at the hands of capitalists and parasites, and to put an end to the starvation which the people had endured. The rural population was divided into three classes: kulaks, who had formerly owned more than seventy-five acres, against whom a merciless campaign was advocated; owners of medium-sized farms who, it was announced, would be tolerated on probation, and landless peasants.

On July 23rd all banks, industrial enterprises, mines and means of transport were nationalized too, and the legal infrastructure was ready for the far more drastic 'reforms' to come. It was unlikely that the few foreign diplomats still remaining in Riga, absorbed as they were in the business of moving out, took much account of these measures, but the future of the Baltic States was clearly grim.

With only two more days to go before the deadline we telegraphed again to London begging for instructions, though it was clearly too late for us to get away before our privileges were withdrawn. Following an appeal to the Russian authorities we were given grudging permission to stay until August 25th, at our own risk.

CHAPTER 17

On July 22nd President Ulmanis was carried off to Moscow and his place was taken by a Russian appointee. 'Latvia is dead,' said Lotte.

We now no longer had a single foreign colleague in Riga. On the first morning of our isolation, as we left home, two heavily built characters stepped out from beneath the plane trees and followed us, twenty paces behind, until we reached the Raina Boulevard. As we went into the Consulate, they settled down on a bench in the gardens opposite. There was no attempt to disguise their surveillance. Not *bad* tradecraft, but no tradecraft at all. We wondered whether they would stay on all day or be relieved by another pair, since we now usually worked until ten or eleven at night.

The walk along the Canal to the office had ceased to be a pleasure. The parks, no longer refreshed by the firemen's hoses, looked parched and dusty, and on the trees the leaves were beginning to wither.

The very sound patterns of the city had changed. Each morning at 5 a.m. squadrons of Russian planes, flying low, roared over the house tops, adding to this unwelcome awakening a feeling of dread. Troops marched constantly through the streets, some singing in wonderful deep-throated voices the Red Army marching songs—an echo of the German troops in Vienna who had so often woken us to the sound of *'Heute gehort uns Deutschland, Morgen die ganze Welt'*.

Loudspeakers had been fitted to the lamp posts at strategic points in the streets. All day long they blared out Communist propaganda varied by monotonous repetitions of the *Internationale*.

One morning we walked through the harbour and along the quays to the office, followed by our shadows, who may even have appreciated a little change of itinerary. A Russian cruiser and some gun boats were tied up alongside, the sailors all lined up on deck and doing P.T. The flags on the few Latvian ships had been replaced by red ones. When shipping was nationalized on July 23rd all Latvian vessels had been recalled to their home ports but only a few had returned. This the Russians tried to remedy by putting pressure on the owners and threatening the relatives of the crews. Failure to return was categorized as sabotage, punishable by twenty-five years forced labour.

On August 5th the Supreme Soviet granted the 'requests' of the puppet governments of the Baltic States, and Latvia, Estonia and Lithuania became respectively the 14th, 15th and 16th Socialist Republics of the Soviet Union. Each delegate spoke in his own language, lip service to the myth that Lenin's proposal of self-determination for subject peoples had been realized. After the 1918 Revolution it had seemed that Russia proper would consist of an area of about two-thirds of the former Tsarist empire, in which roughly half the population spoke Russian. The other language groups were to be granted autonomy within a loose federation. The western borderlands, Finland, the Baltic States and Poland had, between the wars, achieved real independence. Now, they too had lost their freedom.

Until this moment the Russians considered that they had handled the Latvians with kid gloves. But the brief honeymoon was over. Latvia must be brought into line with the Soviet Union of which it now formed a part. The clocks were put back to accord with Moscow time, three hours behind GMT. Latvian currency would be withdrawn. From now on it was forbidden to lay flowers on the National War Memorial. Traditional Latvian dress was no longer to be worn.

Official looting began in earnest. Whole warehouses were emptied; chemists' shops and hospitals stripped bare. Machinery of all sorts was seized. Livestock, fodder, food grains and timber were carried off to Russia. All the more modern railway trucks and carriages were taken in exchange for decrepit Russian rolling stock on a tonnage ratio, that is to say three Baltic 17-ton cars were exchanged for one Soviet 50-ton unit. These trucks were far too large for Latvian traffic.

As in Russia, at that time, trade unions were abolished. Communist dogma maintained that in a Socialist community the relations between workers and management were not, as in a capitalist state, the relations between buyers and sellers of labour. The obligations and rights of workers in a Socialist State were predetermined by a working contract, so there was no longer any need for workers' organizations, which were merely a survival from former class struggles. The Latvian workers were now effectively shackled.

Under the new regime, the funds to which workers and their employers had formerly contributed had been nationalized, and no one would be entitled to draw the benefits for which they had saved.

It had been the custom for men to down tools and clean up so that they were ready to leave the factory when the hooter went. This life style came abruptly to an end and workers were forbidden on pain of fines and even more unpleasant measures, to leave their benches until time was up. Latvians were clean people. That in itself was fair enough, but if they were to indulge in a good wash on factory premises, it must be in their own time, and as long as the soap lasted.

Ironically, an order for cleanliness in factories was the subject of one of the endless compulsory meetings called by the People's Commissar for Light Industry and advertised in the *Russkaya Gazeta*. These meetings were described as 'social events' but were compulsory, even though the theme of many did not apply to the up-to-date conditions hitherto obtaining in Latvian factories. Those who failed to turn up were listed as politically unreliable.

The most hated innovation was the Labour Book, a system used in the Soviet Union. Each book contained a worker's complete record and was as vital to him as his internal passport. Any misdemeanours were noted, and a man could not move to a new job without producing a signed permission from his former employer or supervising commissar, who could withhold consent without giving any reason.

Strikes for any cause whatever were forbidden.

It is not surprising that the processions organized to celebrate the entry of Latvia into the Soviet Union lacked enthusiasm. This time the demonstrators were marched along under escort and the processions were thickly seeded with AGITPROP men from Russia. Some of the marchers bore sheets of plywood daubed with portraits of Communist leaders. Others had nailed bunches of flowers to scrawled placards. Four men were carrying an oleograph of Stalin in a brass frame mounted on poles, which had probably been looted from some church. A few of the marchers were singing, reading the words from scraps of paper. To liven up this rather dreary demonstration, the procession was interspersed with military bands.

My reading sessions with Our Friend had been extended to include the *Russkaya Gazeta* which, unlike *Pravda* and *Izvestia,* contained all the local news. This made our work more interesting, since besides our usual scanning for items of industrial and military interest from all over the Soviet Union, we were able to look for news which might intimately concern us.

For instance, it was proposed to settle one million Russians in Latvia, increasing the population by fifty per cent. Armed forces personnel and functionaries were pouring into Riga and accommodation had to be found for them, so a drastic reorganization of the housing situation would be required. The *Gazeta* announced that the Russian housing norm of nine square metres per head was to be introduced into the Baltic States.

'Just a moment,' I said to Our Friend. 'I *must* tell my husband.'

Kenneth looked up with a sigh from the coding book, but he was at once alert. 'Every room, including kitchens, bathroom, halls, passages and larders will be included in the total space to be divided,' I explained. He was scribbling on the back of an envelope.

'That will mean thirteen people in our flat,' he said.

'Requisitioning starts today,' I added. 'And our official privileges ceased ten days ago.'

'It's time we thought of moving.'

On arriving home we found Lotte in tears.

'Is your old mother worse?' we asked.

'Oh she's all right. She'll be gone. The doctor says she won't live long enough to suffer as we shall.' Her face brightened at this comforting thought, but quickly clouded. 'It's my life savings. The Russians have stolen all but a thousand Lats (about £50). Nationalized, they call it. All my life I've worked for nothing.' I held her hand while she cried quietly.

The country was now being flooded with worthless roubles which the new arrivals could exchange at a very favourable rate against the Lat. Official assurances to the contrary, the Latvian currency was being rapidly devalued. In their panic, people rushed to buy whatever they could find, without pausing to consider what they could do with it. The Russian immigrants, astonished by the abundance even in the now sadly depleted shops, competed for the most unlikely articles.

In an attempt to check the headlong spending, which had already served its purpose in reducing almost to nil the consumer goods available, a regulation was introduced condemning 'speculation', which could be taken to mean almost any kind of purchase. Speculators were tried and, when convicted, given sentences of from five to ten years' imprisonment. Judges who refused to pass sentence for a petty offence were attacked in the press and frequently dismissed.

There was talk of introducing the death penalty, as in Russia, for those convicted of speculation. But in spite of penalties, present or future, the buying fever did not abate.

The State Pawn Shop had played an important part in Riga life. Apart from its conventional function it had assumed the role of a reputable antique shop and one went there to buy Russian silver ikons and all the relics of a generation of emigrés. It had also served as a completely trustworthy valuation agency. Before selling a piece of jewellery, or even having it repaired, one would take it to the pawn shop for a certificated description and valuation, which was never disputed. The *Russkaya Gazela* now announced that any item in the pawn shop worth more than three hundred Lats, or fifteen pounds, would be confiscated. With all but a residue of its stock seized and the death penalty hovering over any unapproved form of buying and selling this wonderful old institution was doomed.

CHAPTER 18

The requisitioning parties had now reached the top of our road. Since we no longer enjoyed Consular protection we should be evicted like everyone else. Many families, nervous about the happenings in Riga, had stayed on at the Strand. If a flat was empty, the troops merely broke down the front door and made a rapid job of throwing books and ornaments out of the window. If an owner returned in time, he could collect what remained of his treasures from the street below.

Unless we took immediate action our home would go the same way as the rest, so we decided to sell up. Office funds were running low since the banks, now nationalized, could no longer change cheques, so the money from our sale would be useful, and later we would be credited with it in London.

Work in the Passport Control Office was more demanding than ever, and we would not be able to return home during office hours. Lotte could not be expected to cope with buyers on her own, so we put an advertisement on the office door. 'Entire contents of No. 14/4 Ausekla iela for sale on August 14th at 7.30 p.m.' Speed was essential and there was no time to haggle with individual buyers.

Tom Brimelow [Later, Lord Brimelow, Head of the Foreign

Office], the Vice-Consul left in charge, meanwhile, having packed up the Hobson's furniture and sent it to Stockholm for eventual transport to Havana, had settled into their almost empty flat in the Elizabetes iela, and invited us to share it with him. The troops were only a couple of blocks away from us now, but with luck we should conclude our sale in time.

On the Wednesday evening, when we came back from the office, the queue outside our front door stretched right down the stairs and out into the street, and we had some difficulty in persuading people that we were not queue-bashers as we struggled to reach our flat. As Lotte opened the front door the crowd forced its way in with us. Lotte had been well coached and confined herself to the duties of a security officer, standing squarely by the front door to see that nothing was stolen. We each took a different room and all through the long evening repeated over and over again, 'No. I'm sorry, but we can't sell things separately. Everything or nothing.'

Round about ten o'clock a young couple, hoping to get married shortly, walked in with a roll of notes.

'May we have your things? We shall treasure them. Perhaps this will help you a little to bear their loss. We will come and fetch them tomorrow—a little at a time if, you don't mind.'

We sat round the dining room table with Lotte for the last time and drank hot tea with strawberry jam in the old Russian way which she loved. We were tired and shaken and Lotte dabbed at her eyes with the corner of her apron.

Next morning, her black coat buttoned tightly round her in spite of the weather, with Vufi and the plants travelling as usual in the oilcloth bag, Lotte waddled away out of our lives, followed by FIX and FAX, carrying her tin box and some oddments rolled up in the crocheted counterpane.

The bundle of Lats was accepted, as promised, by the

Consulate and many months later, in London, we received a cheque for £200.

Once more we were homeless. For the second time we had seen a country invaded and disrupted, and the suffering that this brought. But whereas in Vienna the Jews had born the brunt of the German annexation and the tenure of daily life continued more or less the same, in Latvia there was a total downgrading of the environment. For most people it was the end of the pleasant life they had struggled to build up and the death of their hopes.

The effect of the two takeovers might be compared with that of a man attacking a meadow with a scythe, or one flattening it with a bulldozer.

We now settled in to a strange spartan life in the Hobsons' empty flat. Each of us had a camp bed, a kitchen plate, cup, glass, spoon, knife and fork. Tom pinned a Union Jack on the front door and a notice saying that the flat was the property of the British Consulate and enjoyed extra-territoriality. His Russian was excellent as, before joining the Foreign Service as a probationary vice-consul in Danzig, he had taken his interpreters hip with distinction after only nine months' study.

Food was becoming scarce, partly as a result of the depredations of the Russians and partly due to the disruption caused by the nationalization of the land. An anti-*kulak* campaign was under way, bringing a chilling reminder of the great famine in Russia. The word *kulak* originally meant a dishonest middle man who lived by battening on the labour of others. Having been used as a term of abuse in the early post-Revolution days it gradually broadened its meaning to cover all those peasants who were capable and independent enough to be a threat to the Communist way of life. The extermination of the best of the peasant stock was now under way in the Baltic States.

Supremely indifferent to logic and intent on collectivization, the authorities drove home, through the media, the fact that the small farming units which they themselves had created were not large enough to be viable. At the same time, an intensive propaganda campaign on behalf of the *kolkhozes* or collective farms began to appear in the press. Collective farming was contrary to the deepest instincts of the Latvian peasants, who had yearned for generations to possess the land which was to be theirs for so short a time. Apathy set in and the peasants began to slaughter their livestock.

The supply of food was further hindered by the shortage of transport. Spare parts and tyres were almost unobtainable, so the number of vehicles in service decreased steadily, while the needs of industry and the towns were given priority over the countryside. In an attempt to fill the gap, those car owners in the rural areas whose vehicles had not yet been nationalized were obliged to act as public carriers. Cars were commandeered and used without bothering to inform the owners. They, on the other hand, were obliged to keep the vehicles road worthy in order to avoid a charge of sabotage, and received in return arbitrary payments which were usually quite inadequate.

'Transport's always been a headache in Russia,' said Glyn Hall. 'Thornton, the Metropolitan Vickers man who spent years in Russia, told me that the Nizhni Novgorod car factory had turned out too many right-handed mudguards, but rather than hold up production they fitted only one to each vehicle and sent them off to remote parts of Russia.'

In fact, there had been a self-criticism piece in *Pravda* a few days before about vehicles with missing parts.

The Russians were now requisitioning the houses in the Elizabetes iela. Next morning we were startled by a thunderous knock on the front door. A corporal and half a dozen men were standing outside. 'Tom,' we called.

'You have one hour in which to leave,' said the corporal. He clearly expected no argument. Tom pointed to the Union Jack and the notice beside it.

'This flat is extra-territorial,' he said firmly. 'You may not enter.' His assured manner and fluent Russian made up for his youthful appearance.

The corporal was nonplussed. Here was something not covered by his orders and it might be wiser to act cautiously. He turned to the men. 'Up to the fourth floor,' he said sharply. The sound of a pistol butt battering the panels of the door above echoed down the stair well.

We had now settled, with Tom, into a simple domestic rhythm. Each morning we drew up our hard wooden chairs round the folding card table and drank our 'coffee'. Regularly, before we left the office, the requisitioning squad, headed now by a captain, would knock on the door and demand entry.

Bravely faced by Tom, they would argue the extra-territorial question and finally go away to report the failure of their mission. Soldiers were being billeted all through the block at a ratio of ten men to one room, sleeping on the floor. At this rate we were depriving about sixty men of a hard bed, while we three enjoyed the luxury of a whole empty flat. Clearly we were behaving like bloated capitalists, even though our domestic equipment conformed to the Soviet socialist norm. At any moment the requisitioning squad might have orders to evict us, so we were careful to keep nothing compromising in the flat. When the cleaning woman hung torn up strips of *Russkaya Gazeta* in the loo, we prudently replaced it with *Briva Zeme*.

News of the Battle of Britain had been coming over the radio. In the *Rigascher Rundschau* we had read horrible descriptions of the bombardment of Poland, France, Belgium and Holland by the Luftwaffe. Seen from outside, and to judge from my mother's brave but ill-founded certainties, England was tiny and alone, and unaware of the odds against her. Anxiously, we decided to let the arrangements for the boys' journey to America go ahead.

Though the burden of visa work was reaching its climax, ciphering at least was eased. Now that the balloon had gone up and sovietization was taking its predictable course, there seemed less point in sending telegrams to London, especially since, in view of the continued silence as to our future movements, we felt some doubt whether our messages were being read. Our Friend had long abandoned his natty suits and now slipped into the back door of the office in a variety of scruffy clothing, sometimes carrying a bag of tools.

'We're cutting down on telegrams,' I told him, 'and we'll only report anything of very special interest.' So we scanned the papers carefully and spent the rest of the time chatting.

Our Friend's brother, who worked in the Latvian Intourist office, had made frequent trips to Russia in the past and brought back all sorts of reports.

'People become very ingenious when they're hard-pressed,' Our Friend told me one day. 'When my brother was in Moscow he heard about a clandestine queue club. Some bright person had the idea of organizing a shopping intelligence service. Members were given tip-offs about where some foodstuff or other would be for sale. In return, they had to hand over ten per cent of what they had been able to buy. They then got the password for the following day, in exchange for which they would get further information. But the authorities got wind of it and made an example of the organizers. Twenty years in a labour camp, I think it was. You'll see queues everywhere in Russia, sometimes forming in space, probably because of a rumour, true or false. There was a useful reservation system too.'

'What was that?'

'Just a number chalked on your back, so that you could hurry from one queue to another and find your place reserved when you returned.'

'What about the easy divorce one heard so much about?'

'That's not quite so popular now. A husband has to give his ex-wife one-third of his salary. One chap my brother knew had been married three times. When he took a fourth wife he was obliged to live on her alimony as the whole of his salary was already forfeit.'

'And supposing the husband was unemployed?'

'When my brother was last there unemployment was officially non-existent. This avoided the need for unemployment pay—a considerable economy. It also looked good on paper.'

I asked if this was still going on.

'I can't say, but in any case you won't see any unemployed or undesirables in a first-class zone like Moscow. You can't even spend a night there without having your internal passport stamped by the police.'

'And is it true that the 1923 famine and the famines in the '30s were deliberately engineered?'

'A certain amount was due to mismanagement and the hatred of the peasants for the collective farm system, but the Soviet leaders set out quite deliberately to crush the opposition of the peasants by mass arrests and deportation, and the commandeering of their remaining foodstuffs. There are no official figures but an estimate of five million deaths in the famine of 1933 is not denied by the authorities. As Lenin said, "With a population of a hundred and forty millions, a few million more or less make no difference at all." The deaths may not have worried them, but the resulting chronic food shortage in the whole of Russia certainly did, though it was too late by then to find an easy remedy.'

'Did the news get through to the outside world?'

'Journalists were excluded from the famine areas, but of course it couldn't be completely hushed up. The American Relief Association, in 1923, sent enough grain to Russia to feed several million people. At the same time the Russians were cynically exporting grain. I myself saw American grain coming in through the port of Ventspils and being loaded into empty trucks which had just taken Russian grain to the harbour for shipment to the Ruhr. You see, it's hard for decent people to credit such callous inhumanity. In fact, they don't *want* to, and that suits the Russians. Do you think that when the same thing happens here the West will attempt to take action?'

The problem of the British colony and its future was becoming acute. Anyone without roots in Riga had already left, but there was a group of people, independent business men or families, like the Whishaws, who had lived in the region for generations. They had weathered the 1918 Revolution by moving to the Baltic States, and in some cases their entire worldly possessions were now concentrated in Latvia and they had no ties in England. Somehow, they hoped, they could cling on.

HMG advised very strongly against any British subject attempting to remain, and a scheme had been proposed to send all the men to Palestine where, presumably, they would join the British forces, and the women to Murmansk for a problematical onward journey by sea. It was not clear whether the Russians had agreed to this idea.

One evening, feeling tired and depressed, we decided to leave the office at nine and go to a cinema. Only Soviet films were now on show and the choice lay between 'Lenin and the October Revolution' which we had already seen; 'The Mannerheim Line', which would be far too painful; 'Life on a

Kolkhoz', and the achievements of a Stakhanovite worker in a textile mill, which was showing in a nearby flea pit. We chose the textile worker, knowing from experience that the sound would be blurred by the rustling of sunflower seed husks. The seeds were very popular with the more modest audiences, who split them with their front teeth, swallowed the kernel and spat the husk neatly onto the floor, to form a carpet which crunched at every movement. The noise was apt to mar love scenes and dramatic moments, but would pleasantly dim the drone of propaganda which was bound to take up a large proportion of the film.

For two hours we watched the heroine running from loom to loom in order to beat the quota. By the end of the film she was running so fast that even the audience felt tired and breathless. Her reward, after an endless harangue by a commissar from Moscow, was a firm handshake and a very frizzy perm, which puzzled the audience, as a permanent wave had not yet become an unattainable luxury in Riga.

Our shadows, who seemed as thick mentally as their boots, stuck glumly to their brief and to the bench opposite the Consulate front door, and apparently took no interest in what went on at the back of the office.

There were moments when the presence of these heavy-footed fellows became almost intolerable. We were too busy to lose time in a serious attempt to free ourselves of their surveillance so, being stuck with them, we began to take a mild interest in their welfare. Hobson's flat was nearer the office than the Ausekla iela, just a walk through the leafy Vermana Park and the length of a block, so our shadows spent more time than ever on the bench.

'Just imagine sitting there for thirteen or fourteen hours with nothing to do,' I said to Kenneth. 'It must be terribly boring for them. Don't you think we might say "Good morning" and "Good evening"? Perhaps we could offer them a cigarette.'

Finally, like shy bovine creatures, they approached and accepted an occasional fag, provided no one else was in sight.

CHAPTER 19

There were now only five days to go until we were supposed to leave the country, and still no word from London. It was clear that our official activities were at an end, so we posted a notice on the Consulate door that after August 20th the Passport Control Office would be closed to the public.

With a successful sale behind us we decided that HMG should also have the chance of profiting from our commercial activities, so once more we put up a notice announcing, this time, the sale of our office effects.

On Tuesday, 20th the outer office was full of despairing visa applicants whose hopes of escaping from Latvia were vanishing. The next day the same office was crowded with people of a different sort, bundles of notes in their hands, grasping at chairs, desks, stationery, typewriters, the office clock, a battered map of Riga and the Russian and Latvian dictionaries. From the depths of our cupboards the strangest things emerged—an abacus with one row of beads missing, a dented samovar, a Mazzawattee tea tin. Everything found a buyer, including our show piece, an old typewriter which, if one wedged it skilfully with an india rubber and depressed the return lever, would send the whole carriage whizzing into a waste-paper basket, strategically placed, below.

This we had used to divert our colleagues in the days when the pace of life had been easier.

In mid-morning there was a startled hush as a Russian officer, in uniform, strode in at the door. It seemed however that he too was a purchaser and, by implication, not out to chase speculators. After fingering a round ebony ruler and running his eye over the roll-top desk, he made for an archaic typewriter which we had found on the top shelf of a cupboard. This machine was so old-fashioned that it had no shift key, but eight rows of Russian characters, with capital and ordinary letters on separate keys. This gave it an impressive appearance, apparently superior in his eyes to the four rows of keys on a modern machine. Just for a lark we named a stiff price and, without comment, he counted out the notes, gathered up the machine and went off with it. An hour later all we had left was essential equipment, the codes and the office armoury.

Having done our duty by the government and raised enough money to pay the office light and telephone bills, we could concentrate on our arrangements for the journey.

Paul would be leaving Riga with his parents and the rest of the British colony. His work had come to an end, so we had a farewell party in the office with vodka and fruit juice and some sticky cakes made by his mother.

We had now to reach a decision about our route. The journey to Odessa was straightforward and would take us comparatively quickly out of Russia, but the onward connections to Bombay and Durban and round the Cape were impossible to ascertain.

The Trans-Siberian Express normally ran from Moscow to Dairen, but the route lay through Manchukuo, and the nearest visa-issuing authority for that country was in Berlin. Charles Orde's passport had been sent to Berlin eleven months after we were at war with Germany and returned duly visaed, but this had taken time, and that was something we didn't have.

Our Friend, helpful as usual, put us in touch with his brother in the Latvian Intourist office who came up, next morning, with the good news that there was an outbreak of plague in Manchukuo, causing the Trans-Siberian Express to be diverted to Vladivostok. But Vladivostok was a naval base and had been closed to unauthorized persons for the last twenty years. It remained to be seen whether the Russians would allow us to go there.

Our Intourist contact also produced the unwelcome information that we should not be allowed to take any roubles with us on the journey and that every requirement, including fares, the cost of hotel accommodation, meals, drinks, porters at each stage of the journey, transport to and from the hotels in Moscow and Vladivostok and any amenities we might hope to secure, must be listed in triplicate and paid in advance in gold dollars. This arbitrary gold dollar would more than treble the bill. He said also that we would not be allowed a choice of hotels, but must specify whether we wanted first-, second- or third-class accommodation.

'I thought classes had been abolished in Russia,' I protested, 'and that on the train one travelled "hard" or "soft".'

'Not since 1937,' he replied and, lowering his voice, 'you will find much more emphasis on class in Russia than here. You'd better apply for a first-class hotel in Moscow, but ask for third-class in Vladivostok. There's only one hotel in Vladivostok, and it's terrible. Why payout twenty-two gold dollars a day for first-class accommodation when all you will get is no better than third-class, costing twelve?'

Friends in the American Embassy who had made the east–west journey the year before had told us that the food on the train was uneatable and the water positively dangerous. 'We took two crates of gin bottles filled with boiled water,' they said, 'and tins and cartons of food for the whole journey.' It seemed that we would be wise to do the same.

So we made out our applications, including such trivia as the cost of some picture postcards and newspapers, but excluding any food on the train. The final bill would include a compulsory charge of one gold dollar a head per day for 'sightseeing', though why they should charge for the view from the train windows we could not imagine.

To pay for all this we had to open the Sealed Fund, a large envelope of money issued to offices abroad for just such an emergency. With the applications in and the money ready, we set to work to collect food and water for the journey. Down in the cellar we found the empty gin bottles and packing cases we needed and assembled them in the outer office.

With the help of Our Friend's black market connections our store of tins, some of them containing smoked lampreys and sour cucumbers and other less usual picnic fare, gradually mounted, and we were feeling optimistic when news reached us that, according to an edict just issued, no food might be taken from Latvia across the old White Russian frontier.

It was an invariable rule than an application to make a journey, which had to be sanctioned by the NKVD besides the Ministry of Transport in Moscow, once made, could not be changed. If we devoured a large packed meal this side of Vitebsk we could hold out until Moscow, but we were then faced with ten days in the Trans-Siberian without food. Our only hope was to throw ourselves on the mercy of the Moscow Embassy, but we had no idea how they were placed for stores. We only knew that they were short of currency.

While we were considering our unhappy position we heard from Our Friend's brother that the whole of the Latvian Intourist staff had been sacked with effect from the next day. 'I will see that your applications get lost,' his message went. 'Make out fresh ones, including food on the train, and allowing yourselves several days in Vladivostok as no one can tell how you will get on to Japan from there.'

Our party would consist of Co Froebelius and his wife Barbara, Nick and Dorothy, and ourselves. If all went well, we should have six first-class berths on the Trans-Siberian Express from Moscow on Wednesday, September 4th.

Apparently, though the import of food was not allowed, the Russians had no objection to drink of any sort being brought over the former frontier, so we collected the last of our stocks and packed a strange collection of odds and ends, including tomato and celery juice and anything whatever containing alcohol, into a small crate.

But this tolerance did not extend to clothing, and to our dismay we were issued with a printed sheet laying down the norm to which we had to conform. Each man could take with him two suits, one overcoat, a change of underclothes, two shirts, one sweater, three pairs of shoes and a pair of goloshes.

The official imagination did not run to frivolities like ties and scarves. The norm for women ran along the same lines. We decided each to pack a case containing the norm, but to try our luck with the rest of the luggage, including things to be sold in Moscow.

The morning this bombshell hit us we had just returned to the flat when the front door bell rang and Herr Schonberg tottered into the hall carrying an immensely heavy parcel.

'A small token of the gratitude of the Jewish Agency for all you have done for my people,' he announced, his sad old face lighting up.

We undid the wrappings to reveal an immense cut-glass bowl rimmed with silver. It was filled with beautiful hothouse grapes, something rarely seen even in the happy days in Riga. The present, and the old man's heroic effort in bringing it, were deeply touching and we enjoyed the grapes, but felt it was hardly likely the Russians would allow us to take such an emblem of bourgeois life-style with us.

Picturing the long days in the train and the stark conditions forecast, even in the first-class, Kenneth and I went on a foraging expedition to the Legation. Although the building was, in theory, extra-territorial it was clear that unless some miracle occurred it was lost to Great Britain. In the half light behind closed shutters we wandered through the familiar rooms. No sale had been organized here, and the Office of Works interior decoration, all polished mahogany and turkey carpets, remained as yet sedately undisturbed.

On a shelf in the Minister's room was an old copy of the Times Atlas. We asked the Chancery Messenger still in charge of the building to fetch a sharp knife, and we cut out all the maps which might be useful during our journey, covering a course right round the world and bringing us back to England not so very far from where we now stood.

We took a supply of pencils and paper and a couple of packs of cards to help pass the time, but the most valuable find was a stock of toilet paper, fine firm Bronco with GOVERNMENT PROPERTY stamped on every sheet.

'This will be ideal for the journey,' I said. 'Not just in the obvious way, but we can use it for scoring at cards, and to clean up our carriage and write little notes to each other, and to wipe our fingers if the water in the hand basin runs out. There's no end to its usefulness. Each of us can hang a roll from our shoulder by a loop of string. The rest we'll stuff into odd corners in the luggage.'

So we took a couple of dozen rolls from the store cupboard and bowled them across the polished floor of the Chancery to the entrance hall, where the Chancery Messenger gathered them up and put them into a Foreign Office Bag.

We found some more treasures in the Chancery bookshelf—a copy of Murray's Guide to Russia of 1875, the account by a Swiss surgeon, Hans Jakob de Fries, of his journeys through Siberia between 1774 and 1776, and a copy of *The Rabbit King of Russia* by Reginald Urch. During his years as *Times* correspondent in Moscow before his imprisonment in the Lubyanka Gaol, Urch had forwarded to his paper an extraordinarily detailed record of Stalin's drive to speed up industrialization and collectivize agriculture. After his release and expulsion from Russia he had embodied all the most interesting facts in a novel about a keen young Communist engaged in the rabbit-breeding campaign of the early thirties. Although the story was fictitious, the background was factual and accurately documented in a series of footnotes.

When we had visited Urch at his *dacha* he had shown us one wall of his study lined with files of newspaper cuttings bringing his Russian press records up to date. This treasure was probably lost when Urch was transferred to Helsinki and covered the Finnish War on behalf of the *Times*.

With no more visa clients and few telegrams to send, we now had our evenings to ourselves. While we played patience or marvelled at the oddities described in the 'Rabbit King' Tom, with his dictionaries spread out on the card table, worked tirelessly to extend his knowledge of Russian. There must be very few people who are prepared, hour after hour, to follow through the ramifications of a single word. Starting with a first group of meanings, Tom would look up each of these in turn and repeat the process until his research fanned out over a score of related words. Without his extraordinary memory the exercise might have been just a feat of endurance, but in his case, it was clearly rewarding.

But for the company of Reginald Urch our evenings would have lacked sparkle. As it was, we took it in turns to read his book and tell each other the most amusing bits.

'Rabbitization was part of the Russian Five Year Plan,' said Kenneth. 'According to the Small Soviet Encyclopaedia a pair of rabbits, properly handled, might produce more than a million descendants in four years, and it was calculated that if a ship were half loaded with rabbits in Australia, by the time it reached Odessa of Leningrad it would have a full cargo.

'At the Kraskovo State Rabbit Farm the animals were kept in wire-bottomed cages and moved forward each day, cropping the grass as they went. When they reached the boundary they were shifted back again on a parallel course. After twenty-five days' round trip they should have been ready for skinning and canning. *Izvesria* in April 1932 published a full-page eulogy of the rabbit scheme, but *Pravda* on August 28th announced that seven thousand of the nine thousand rabbits supplied to a new State Farm had died in the first few weeks. Obviously this must be the fault of wreckers. Scapegoats were immediately produced and tried.

'As an example of reprehensible non-eo-operation in such a splendid scheme the *Sorzialislicheskoye Zemledeliye* reported a message received from the director of a large State Farm, "Send no more rabbits. Haven't ordered them, won't take them and don't want any more letters on the subject."

'My turn with the book,' I said. 'This is absolutely fascinating. It looks as though rabbits were only part of a wave of bright ideas for improving food supplies. Listen to this. In January '32 they set up a kangaroo farm in the North Caucasus. The animals were to be used for food, fur and, guess what, ornamental trimmings.

'Then they set to work on a One Year Plan for Emu Culture. Six pairs of emus were to produce sixty eggs of which, due to the colder climate, thirty would be addled. The thirty surviving chicks would be hatched in incubators and then spend the winter in little wooden houses on the Steppes. People who tried emu flesh said that it tasted horrible, but the Soviet press announced that the eggs were very palatable. Each egg would yield about a pound and a half of nourishing meat, but the emus refused to co-operate and went off laying. All this was reported in the *Times* in August 1932.

'In 1933 there was a scheme for making lubricating oil for agricultural machinery from locusts. Then there was the State Beetle-Soap Industry. Bugs and beetles of all sorts were to be used, but it turned out that their bodies didn't contain enough fat.'

'Then there was the pig campaign,' said Kenneth, who had taken his turn with the book. 'This started off with a blaze of publicity. "Pigs must be given pride of place in the Soviet system. The watchword is 'All eyes on the swine.'" But the difficulty was to feed them. Each family was ordered to raise a pig, and the animals were to be used in the cities as auxiliary scavengers. But the owners ate the pigs and the pig food too, and on September 25th, 1930, forty-eight campaign directors and food specialists were shot without trial as saboteurs.

'At the *Petrovsk Kolkhoz* the peasant Krivolok reported that one and a half tons of tadpoles had been fished out of the nearby swamps and offered to the pigs as food. Unfortunately the pigs didn't fancy them until they were boiled into a stew with some goose feet for flavouring. Then each of the animals gobbled up five kilos and soon two hundred and sixty pigs were in prime condition. This was reported in the *Moscow News* of December 24th, 1932. But the tadpoles grew up into frogs and the food supply ceased. The Soviet tadpole industry was not included in the Second Five Year Plan.'

'Listen to this, Tom,' I said. 'This is something really good.' He looked up patiently, one finger marking his place in the dictionary.

'Did you know that the Russians invented a scientific, laboursaving method of chemical sheep-shearing? A Professor Ilyin found that by giving increasing doses of certain "heavy" chemicals to the animals they would shed their fleece in four instalments, automatically graded from the coarsest to the finest wool. He was able to do this up to four times a year, but unfortunately the sheep tended to die young. The same process was tried with the reindeer in the Kola Peninsular. They only produced one coat a year and must have suffered considerably from the cold. Ilyin was made a hero of the Soviet Union.

'And then a story came through that someone had seen a pack of naked wolves racing around in the snow in the neighbourhood of Minsk "to keep warm" as the report said. They had raided the local sheep farm. So people began to wonder if sheep shorn by the new method would be suitable as food . . .'

'You're making it up,' said Tom.

'No, it was all in the Soviet Agricultural Bulletin on October 12th, 1936. They even found they could produce animals with coats of different colours by dosing them with certain chemical and varying the temperatures in which the animals were kept. You won't believe this, but there was actually a reference in the Soviet press to Jacob's success in producing black, white, spotted and piebald sheep and goats to. suit his contract with his future father-in-law. They'll quote the Bible, you see, if it suits them.'

Kenneth was leafing through the book. 'What about the plan to take a daily gallon of blood from all the horses and cattle in the Soviet Union?' he asked. 'They reckoned that with a herd of two hundred cattle one could make up to eleven hundred delicious dishes a day—soup, sausages, "chocolate" and so on, all at a very cheap price.

'And they turned an old warship into a floating factory to catch the dolphins in the Black Sea and make them into sausages. That was in the *Krasnaya Gazeta* as early as July 22nd, 1930. And it failed like the other schemes. All this fun and games because they had killed off the human animals who were making such a far better job of production.' Kenneth snapped the book shut.

Next morning we were all three to be inoculated with TAB, anti-plague and cholera vaccines. Our friend Dr Eichler had disappeared and the Jewish Hospital was closed. We must go to a Russian doctor, newly arrived. Two of the shots were made, as usual, in the arm, but for the third he told us to bare our tummies and, taking a roll of flesh between finger and thumb, thrust a large needle deep in the direction of our hearts. Later, we all felt exceptionally ill and tossed on our camp beds with soaring temperatures.

News was coming through of nightly raids on England. Surely, we felt, the boys would be safer in West Virginia. The Welsh hills might seem safe to my mother, who was apt to measure distances by the time they took to walk, but Cardiff was a target and what were thirty or forty miles to a Heinkel jettisoning its bombs? If only we could foresee what might happen.

The office was already closed to the public when Professor Pekšens knocked on the door.

'I've come to say goodbye,' he said, laying the woollen cap which had replaced his grey Homburg on the counter beside his knitted gloves. He had the dehydrated look of the pet newt I had kept as a child, which had escaped from its bucket in the nursery and been found, days later, tiny and almost transparent under the sofa. I had carefully nursed the newt in a saucer of water, its head supported on a piece of damp blotting paper, and it had recovered. But it never regained the brilliant orange stripes which had been its pride.

'I have been dismissed from the University,' Pekšens said. 'My lectures were politically unsound. I have lost my flat too and I'm going to join my brother and his family in Jelgava. They've been evicted from their flat and gone to live in their *dacha*. It's very small, but even so it exceeds their housing allowance. You see the inspector counted the woodshed as living space. As you know, it would be far too cold in winter to sleep there. According to the authorities they have a vacancy and I must hurry to arrive before they put in a stranger. I am leaving everything here but a few books. I've brought you this . . . Perhaps it will remind you of our happy meetings.'

It was a small, well-thumbed copy of *The Diary of a Nobody* which we had read together. In the margins were notes he had made.

'I'm worried about the Addisons,' said Tom one evening. 'The old lady is determined to stay on here. "I shall die soon," she told me, "so why ship me off who knows where, to be buried in some place not nearly as comfortable as our pine wood. That's where I want to be planted." She's a naughty old pet and serenely unaware of Una's problems.'

'The sacrificial daughter,' I agreed. 'In Victorian families one of the girls was always destined to look after her parents and renounce a life of her own. I'm sure that's why so many women made unsuitable marriages—just to escape.'

The Foreign Office plan to divide the British colony between Murmansk and Palestine had been discarded in favour of a scheme, equally unpopular, to send them all to Petsamo on the Arctic Circle, where a Vice-Consul was waiting to supervise their journey to England—no one knew by what means.

Indignation was reaching fever pitch and a mass determination was building up to stay in Riga and be damned.

'I've called a meeting for tonight,' said Tom, 'at the British Club. We've got to face this thing out. Will you two come and support me?'

Most of the colony were middle-aged to elderly, and used to having things pretty much their own way. Tom, with Kenneth beside him, faced them from the platform while I sat at a small table below.

Tom cannot have been more than twenty-four, with only a couple of years' experience in the Consular Service while Kenneth, not many years his senior, had no experience of Consular work proper. The mood of the meeting was, understandably, ugly.

'Why don't you tell those silly buggers in London that I'm not prepared to send my wife and daughter to Murmansk to be clobbered by the Russians while I wander off to Palestine,' shouted a thickset timber merchant.

'The Murmansk scheme has been dropped,' said Tom quietly.

'And what's this we hear about Petsamo?' challenged an engineer, known as a formidable drinker. 'I suppose you'll let us all freeze together.'

There was an uproar. Tom waited unmoved. 'Young enough to be my grandson,' muttered someone in the back row.

'When you've all settled down I'll tell you what's to be done for the moment,' said Tom. At last there was quiet. 'Now I know that many of you have had roots in these parts for generations, and have built up your businesses afresh after the Revolution. This time it's different. There's no land frontier you can cross to safety. Our country is at war, and encircled. Let us agree that our aim is to return home, and that we must wait patiently until orders come through. Meantime, we must get ourselves organized.'

The audience was now following his words quietly. 'First of all I need the names and addresses of every single British subject who is still in Latvia, so in case you know of anyone who is not at this meeting, will you be good enough to ask them to call at the Consulate as soon as possible. As some of you know, I am there every day making out compensation claims for British residents.

'Now I must ask you to give me the name and address of your next of kin in the UK, and for those of you who will ask to be repatriated at government expense, the name of a guarantor at home who will vouch for your repayment of the fare at a later date. If you come up to the table in turn, Mrs Benton will write these details down.

'About the route, there's no need for me to point out that the choice is limited, meantime it's no good guessing. As soon as there are definite plans you will be informed. After all, we are a very small group and our country's position is grave, so we must be patient and keep calm.'

After this, people filed quietly up to the table. The mood of the meeting had changed completely. People were wringing Tom's hand, as well they might, we thought.

Two days before we left I went round to Intourist to collect our tickets and was met with a blank refusal. The new Russian staff were uncooperative and surly.

'You ask for first-class accommodation in Moscow and third-class in Vladivostok. Why?'

'Because . . . hotels are very expensive. We haven't got a lot of money.' I hoped that this non-capitalist approach might soften the official a little, and I couldn't give the true reason. Too late I realized that it might have been wiser to pay the higher price.

'In any case, you can't have the tickets.'

It appeared that these could not be issued without a countersignature from Commissar Agranov of the NKVD, and the commissar had already left his office. Next day was the Soviet Day of Rest and offices would be closed. If the reservations were not taken up at once we should lose them, and our applications would become null and void. It was doubtful whether the Russians would allow us to make another attempt and in any case, the money we had paid over would be lost, and we had no more. The Sealed Fund was almost used up and would only serve to liquidate last-minute expenses.

'Where does the commissar live?' I asked. I was almost in tears. Without answering, the man turned on his heel and disappeared into his office.

'Marijas iela 52, down by the station. Take these.' The girl clerk thrust a bundle of forms into my hand and bent over her typewriter. I hurried out. A tired-looking woman opened the door of the commissar's flat.

'Is Commissar Agranov at home? May I have a word with him?' Through the half-open door of the dining room I could see two children playing in the corner and a man in shirt sleeves sitting at the table. A uniform jacket hung over the chair. The woman gave an uneasy glance at the broad back.

'What is it?' tne commissar called. 'Send her in.'

I explained in my halting Russian our dilemma. 'We've been told to leave. We want to leave'. We *must* catch the train . . . All we need is your signature. *Please.*'

He held out his hand for the papers and looked them through with agonizing slowness. The two children had stopped playing and were crowding to the table. The smaller one climbed up on his knee.

'I have two young boys at home . . .' I ventured.

Without speaking, the commissar drew a massive brass inkwell towards him and scrawled his signature on each form.

'*Spassibo.* Oh, thank you,' I said.

He nodded gravely and I hurried away.

We now had just two problems to settle. We must devise a code for Our Friend, who had volunteered to send messages to London using the wireless set which had been hidden, for possible emergency use, in his nat, and we must dispose of the weapons lying in the safe.

The code would have to be based on books which might be found in any home in Riga. We decided on the standard Brockhaus German dictionary, as our friend spoke no English and his messages would have to be transmitted in German. They would consist of five-figure groups, the first three digits of which would give the page from which a word had been taken, page seven for example being shown as 007, page 25 as 025 and pages from 100 onwards being given entire. The last two digits would show the position of the word, counting from the left hand top corner of each page of the dictionary.

German is a ponderous language and for a time we were at a loss how to simplify it, until we hit on the device of putting all verbs in the infinitive, prefixing them with a standard group, 81111 to indicate the past tense and 82222 to show the future (Brockhaus page numbering stopped at 727). A noun would be modified by a preceding 91111 if it was to be plural.

Having ciphered the message in this way, Our Friend would recipher it using the Riga telephone book with its five-figure numbers. Copies of the local telephone book had been sent to London as a matter of routine.

Our Friend was delighted with the code, and we found on our return to England that messages had come through, though soon there was silence.

The disposal of our armoury presented a different type of problem. This consisted of a Webley & Scott .45 automatic and a Colt .22 with fifty rounds of ammunition each. The discovery of these, even after we had left the office, might lead to trouble. After a careful recce of the surrounding neighbourhood we decided that our best chance lay in dropping the guns into the Canal, provided we could shake our 'shadow'. Fortunately, we had now been demoted to a single escort, and from time to time he would vanish for a moment or two from the bench, perhaps to snatch a bite of food or a drink, or for some other vital purpose, but his absences were unpredictable.

The Canal was crossed by a small bridge almost opposite the office. Kenneth had an old trench coat, the pockets of which opened on the inside and were accessible through a slit from without. There was a chill in the air now as dusk was falling, and the coat would not attract attention. We could see from the window of the Consulate if the 'shadow' left his post. As soon as this happened, we sauntered out and into the gardens, Kenneth with his hands in his pockets. As we crossed the bridge we stopped for a moment and Ie ant on the rail. With a gentle splash the two guns slipped into the water.

The streets of Riga were provided with plentiful drains to take off the snow water and their grids were fitted with widely spaced bars. As we walked along the Elizabetes iela towards the flat we dropped a few bullets onto each grid, being careful to kick any strays down into the drain.

The train left for Moscow at 6.30 p.m. the next day, and this was our last evening in Riga. Before closing the office we had telegraphed to London to say that we were burning our codes at twelve noon the following day. After this, all communication with Head Office would be cut.

CHAPTER 20

Next morning we unlocked the office for the last time and sat uneasily in Nick's room while the hands of our watches moved towards twelve o'clock. The die was cast, as our escape route could not be altered, but it would be comforting to know that if London had not approved our plans, they had at least not issued contrary orders.

A fire was burning in the stove. The code books and reciphering tables lay on the desk. Twelve o'clock struck. We were silent. There was something terribly final about severing the umbilical cord.

At this moment Glyn Hall came in with a telegram.

'I suppose we'd better decipher it,' said Nick.

Word by word the message emerged. 'Head of station to proceed with Corrie to Stockholm. Bentons to go forthwith to Helsinki.' The telegram had come too late. Tearing up the thick code books so that they would burn more easily we put them, together with the telegram, on the fire and watched while they slowly charred and crumbled.

Through the good offices of Our Friend's brother we contacted one of the few Latvian customs officials who had not yet been replaced by a Russian and he agreed that if we could get our luggage to the station during a quiet period in the afternoon, he would 'examine' it and seal it up. FIX and FAX would wait at the customs shed and stow the luggage as soon as the train came in.

That evening we joined the surging crowd at the Moscow Station. A carriage had been reserved for us not, we felt, from courtesy but in order to make sure that we kept ourselves to ourselves.

As the train drew out of the suburbs the sun was setting over the White Lake. Then darkness fell.

CHAPTER 21

We sat disconsolate as the train clanged on through a black void pierced only by occasional lights. The carriage was dirty, the windows grimed. This was Russian rolling stock, part of the compulsory exchange deal with Latvia.

Now we were experiencing the pangs of the refugee that we had so often vicariously felt. We too had lost our roots and were being blown like tumbleweed across the vast expanse of Russia. All that remained of our home was stacked in the racks above our heads. There has been no news of the boys for over three weeks. We had no idea whether they had arrived safely in America or even if they had left Eardisley. Ships were being sunk in the Atlantic, and in England the docks were on fire.

Over twenty-two thousand miles of the journey home lay before us and we were uncertain whether the Russians would allow us to leave the country or whether they would play at cat-and-mouse, arresting us as we were about to leave the Soviet Union.

This they had done to the unfortunate Polish Second Secretary, just as he was stepping into the plane, seen off by the remnants of the diplomatic corps in Riga. During the thirteen days still to go until we reached Vladivostok some adverse discovery by the Russians might seal our fate. Perhaps Our Friend would be picked up with his radio transmitter and his codes, and under pressure he might reveal his connection with us. The light in the carriage was too dim for reading. We sat silent.

Towards midnight the train drew up at an empty station—Bigosovsk—the former frontier with Russia. Lights shone from a large wooden shed at the far end of the platform. The door of our carriage was flung open. A police official pointed to the platform. 'You must get out,' he said. Our luggage was bundled out after us.

'Is this the end of the line for us already?' muttered Nick.

Co Froebelius was talking to one of the police. 'No, it's just a customs examination.'

'But why here? Latvia is part of the Soviet Union now,' I protested. 'Are you sure they're not arresting us?'

'No, look . . .'

To our relief, other people were climbing down onto the platform. The customs shed was filled with anxious passengers, their possessions dumped down indiscriminately. Any luggage without the customs inspector's chalk mark would be left behind, and it was up to us to make sure that ours was examined.

Our crate of drink was opened eagerly by a square-jawed customs official. On top were the remains of our picnic supper, a couple of sandwiches which she quickly slipped under the counter, and some tomatoes. She grabbed these and disappeared. The crowd was thinning as the passengers, their examination completed, drifted back towards the train, which lay immobilized on the rails, the engine breathing heavily and emitting strange noises like an animal asleep.

The woman returned with a more senior official. 'These tomatoes will be confiscated,' he announced.

'*Nichevo,*' we replied. It didn't matter to us. Anything to get on with the examination and back into the train.

'You must have a receipt,' said the woman doggedly. Again she went away. The shed was empty now, and the chilly fear was growing that we might be left behind. All our luggage was unlocked and wide open, spread out on the ample counter.

'*Please* can you look at our things,' we begged. The customs official started to churn through our carefully-packed cases while we struggled to close the lids after him.

'What is this?' he asked, picking up a Snakes and Ladders board, part of our defence against boredom during the journey.

'A game,' we said.

'And this?' He was looking suspiciously at Word Making and Word Taking—a forerunner of Scrabble which we had found at the Hobsons' flat.

'A game too.'

'Only one game,' he said, sweeping the rest under the counter. 'You can keep the playing cards.' Unaccountably, he overlooked Murray's Guide and de Fries's account of his Siberian journey.

The train gave a sudden *Choof, choof,* as if it had woken up and was raring to go. There were no passengers in sight. As I shut my suitcase the official made a grab at a photograph of my father in uniform.

'Who is this?'

'My father,' I replied.

He looked disbelieving, but compared it with an oleograph of Stalin dressed as a Field Marshal which was hanging on the wall of the shed and decided that the snapshot was too casual to be that of a foreign political leader. He dropped it on the counter.

The female customs officer had filled in the receipt and handed it to Kenneth to sign. We still have this and it reads:

'Quarantine inspection at Bigosovsk, 1st September, 1940. Inspector Breusovskaya, acting in accordance with import regulations, completed the following document stating that Mr Benton proceeding to America via Moscow had his baggage examined and the following scheduled plants were found: 11 tomatoes originating in Germany. Signs of disease were noticed (a spotty appearance). The tomatoes were confiscated and destroyed on the customs premises.'

A moment later we were racing for the train as steam hissed out to release the brakes and the engine wheels slowly began to turn. Our luggage was hurled in after us.

The train rumbled on through the darkness, the night bulb in the carriage ceiling shedding only a dim light. I wished that I could sleep like the others, but there comes a time when mind and body are too tired for rest and one remains painfully wakeful. Closed eyes give no relief. There is no escape from merciless awareness. When this happens it is wiser to abandon sleep and remain passive, absorbing any tiny plankton particles of interest which float through the mind.

In the corner opposite us Nick was sleeping, bolt upright, his hair still neatly parted, his toothbrush moustache ending sharply above his lip. His shoes, alone of the party, were still gleaming with years of polish.

On the seat beside him, her head on a rolled-up cardigan, her face looking anxious even in sleep, lay Dorothy Corrie. During our stay at Madame Mossolova's we had shared many meals with Dorothy, as well as working together at the office, yet we had never formed a clear picture of her home background or family ties.

Kenneth and Co Froebelius had settled into opposite corners so that Barbara and I could have something firm to lean against. Barbara was fast asleep on Co's shoulder and his eyes were closed. There were deep hollows beneath the high cheekbones of his pale face and a stubble shadow round his jaw. Perhaps owing to the dominant position of his brother Henry, the archivist, Co had assumed in our eyes a retiring image and, since he was taciturn and in some way alien, none of us had got to know him. Barbara was a handsome dark-haired girl with the quick wits and self-confidence of a Londoner.

Dawn came over a grey landscape. There were no washing facilities and nothing to eat on the train, and in any case, we had no roubles. At Vitebsk a queue formed on the platform for some sort of food, and at Smolensk there was a station buffet from which people emerged looking slightly less depressed. So we consoled ourselves with various mixtures from our crate of drinks and some biscuits which had escaped the attentions of the Breusovskaya. The hours passed very slowly. On the outskirts of Moscow some children were throwing lumps of mud into a muddy stream.

Towards tea time the train drew into the Riga Station, one of the great Moscow terminals. A forceful-looking Intourist courier was coming down the corridor shouting the Russian equivalent of 'Everybody out'. Having assembled a dozen assorted foreigners he collected our Intourist coupons for one porter each, transport to our hotel, the name of which he would not reveal, and also for a sightseeing tour of Moscow.

Outside the station stood a coachful of visibly bored and restive Germans. We wondered how long they had waited for us since their own train came in, but as enemy nationals responsible for the delay felt it wiser not to enquire.

The Intourist guide produced a megaphone. Evidently the sightseeing tour was to be combined with our journey to the hotel. We were driving down a wide street of improbable drabness. 'Workers' flats,' he bawled and then, swinging round to face the other side of the street and with the air of playing a trump card, 'Railway workers' flats'. These buildings, not long completed, had aged before their time and there was nothing to alleviate their sullen proportions and air of dispirited neglect.

'There is a Ten-Year Plan for the city of Moscow,' he bellowed. 'The streets are all to be widened to twenty-five metres. In ten years you will not recognize the city.' This at least held out some sort of encouragement, though we had no wish to check his prophecy.

The coach was taking a direct course towards the centre of Moscow and there were to be no deviations, it seemed, to show us the sights, in spite of our gold-dollar sightseeing coupons. The Germans were indignant, but we were too tired to care. 'But the Kremlin—the Red Square,' protested a burly German.

'You can see them later, if you have time,' he was told with obvious indifference.

Just before we reached the hotel the guide stood up with his megaphone once more. 'That is the office where Molotov works,' he said portentously, pointing to a frowning building. We drew up in front of a large hotel. METROPOL was written over the portico.

'We're twenty-five years too late,' muttered Nick. 'The Metropole was quite something in Tsarist days, I've been told.'

Together with our German companions we were herded through the entrance doors. The foyer was filled with people, mostly German and all querulous. We soon discovered why.

'May we have the key to our room?' we asked at the reception desk.

'Wait here,' was the reply. 'Your luggage has not arrived.'

'We want to go up. The luggage can follow later.'

'You will wait,' said the receptionist with the air of a school mistress addressing an insubordinate child.

Time passed. Everyone was tired in varying degrees and tempers short. To West Europeans the delay was inexplicable. All of us had reservations, otherwise we should not have been there. In one respect we had an edge over the Germans. They, as allies of the Russians, felt entitled to VIP treatment whereas we, from the opposite camp, though not actually at war with Russia, expected to be under-privileged.

More than an hour had passed since we'd reached the hotel and still no one had been allowed upstairs. A massive German woman wearing a fur coat which nearly touched the floor and a toque with a tuft of osprey feathers had been particularly loud in her complaints. When her harassed little husband finally refused to repeat her grievances at the reception desk she announced that she could stand no more. 'I'm going to faint,' she moaned. No one felt strong enough to catch her but, just in time, someone pushed a small gilt chair under her huge behind. This, and the satisfaction of being the only person in the foyer able to sit down, kept her calm for a while.

Two hours passed before we were shown to our room. In Tsarist times it must have been the height of luxury, but the crimson and gold brocade was worn and the carpet had thread-bare patches. An open door led to a large bathroom with over-sized fittings. Wonderful. We could soak in a hot bath and wash off all the grime and fatigue of the journey.

In place of the usual list of hotel regulations on the back of the bedroom door there was a small printed notice.

'Dorothy,' we called, 'does this notice really say what we think it does?'

'Let's see. "Bed linen is changed once in five days irrespective of who sleeps here."'

All three of us hurried to the bed. Sheets and pillow cases were creased and unsavoury with use. It seemed that changing day was near, but not near enough. We rolled the bed linen into a bundle and put it gingerly out in the corridor.

'In the old days in Russia people always travelled with their own sheets,' said Dorothy. 'They thought that using other people's bed linen was as bad as wearing other people's clothes.'

'They may have had something,' Kenneth said.

'I don't see any flecks of blood on the sheets,' said Dorothy consolingly. 'It looks as though there aren't any bugs, at least.'

'If they won't give us clean sheets we can sleep under our coats with a blanket on top,' said Kenneth. 'The room isn't cold. And now, what about that hot bath?'

But the big brass taps, even when turned full on, yielded only a few flakes of rust. There was no water at the hand basin either. We waited in vain for someone to answer the bell and finally washed our hands in the housemaid's cupboard down the corridor.

We had agreed with Nick to meet for dinner in the bar adjoining the dining room, where he was to stand us all a drink on his Intourist coupons. We were hungry, but determined not to worry about the risk of drinking on an empty tummy. There were no guests in the bar, though most of the tables in the dining room were already full. Behind the long mahogany counter and against the rich background of dusty gilded mirrors and carved scrollwork stood an elderly slant-eyed Tartar.

'The Tartars made the best barmen and butlers in the old days,' said Dorothy.

The barman seemed pleased to have some foreign customers and enquired, 'What would the ladies and gentlemen like to drink?'

'Cocktails,' said Nick. 'Dry Martinis.'

'There is no gin. But of course I have vodka.'

Vodka had not, at that time, become a popular substitute for gin, but we decided to try it.

'Wait, I must get the ice,' and the barman hurried away

to return with a large block which he placed on the counter. Fumbling in his pocket he drew out a pair of *pince-nez*, balancing them on his nose, and attacked the ice with an axe, warning us to take cover as he did so. Slivers of ice flew all over the room.

Fatigue and apprehension slipped away as we downed our second and third cocktails and moved over to our table. The dining room was warm with the steamy smells of hot food and not too well washed bodies. Many of the guests were members of the armed forces in neat uniforms, their wives and girlfriends dressed in shiny rayon and printed cotton. Although everyone in the room was, necessarily, privileged, some of the men were wearing open-necked shirts and gym shoes, which struck a discordant note against the opulent, though faded, Tsarist decor.

By now, we were aching with hunger and looking with envy at the plates of *borshtch* and rich-smelling food at neighbouring tables. Nick signalled to a waiter who shouted back '*Seychas*', but in Russia 'at once' only means that your request has been noted and mayor may not be fulfilled.

Eventually, a bowl of caviar and a carafe of vodka appeared. It was so long since our last cocktail that we were quite ready for a follow-up. After venison stew and sticky cakes, accompanied by yet more vodka, and made absolutely delicious by our sharpened appetites, we felt extremely cheerful.

'Let's have an independent sightseeing tour,' said Kenneth.

No one attempted to interfere as we walked out into the street. Most tourists were closely shepherded, but we were an unscheduled group and not yet part of the system. We set out for the Red Square, just round the block, as we had seen from the map in the foyer. The night was sharp with an early frost and the stars huge and brilliant. At this hour the streets were deserted. We skirted a giant hoarding disguising, presumably, some building project, and turned the corner into the square.

It lay before us, vast, empty and silent, bounded on the further side by the high crenellated walls of the Kremlin. Lenin's tomb, a great cube of red and black marble, gleamed darkly under the stars. Behind it, a row of steely-grey conifers lined the base of the walls. For five hundred years these walls had encircled a power-house of despotism. In spite of war and revolution and radical changes of personnel, the autocratic system had remained virtually unchanged.

'Let's go and have a look at Lenin now,' suggested Barbara.

But beside the two motionless sentries was a notice, 'Open from 15 to 18 hours'.

We followed the walls to the great Spasskaya Tower. Sentries with fixed bayonets guarded the entrance which led beneath it into the Kremlin. Co walked calmly up to them. 'Can we come in?' he asked.

The men stood unmoved and Co repeated his question. In those days a tour of the Kremlin was not included in any tourist itinerary and it was probably the only time the sentries had heard such a request. One of the men jerked his head towards the porter's lodge behind him.

'Come on Co,' we said, 'or they'll arrest us on suspicion. They could probably have us for abnormal behaviour.'

Across the square the cathedral of St Basil, with its swirling onion domes patterned in brilliant colour and its gleaming gold pineapple turrets was like some barbaric object washed up on an empty shore.

Fatigue had vanished with the good dinner and the vodka, and the exhilaration of having slipped the lead and roamed free of supervision, even for a short while, but our feet dragged over the last few hundred yards. By the time we reached our bedroom we hardly cared that the sheets still lay in the passage outside our bedroom door.

Next morning the bathroom taps were still dry, so we rang for the chambermaid. After half an hour a woman appeared.

'I am the only maid on this floor,' she said. 'The bath is out of order.'

'Then may we have some hot water and a plug for the basin?'

The latter request clearly puzzled her. (Russians will only wash their hands under a running tap and even in Tsarist times travellers had to bring their own plug or do without.)

After another long wait she returned with a small jug of water and stood with it in her hand.

'Thank you. Please stand it in the basin.'

'It is the only jug on this floor. I must wait for it.'

We conquered our embarrassment and managed to wash under her unblinking stare.

That morning we were to visit the Embassy, where we hoped to borrow some roubles. The day was brilliantly fine and we decided to go on foot, once again, luckily, unaccompanied. Our way took us through Red Square.

Outside Lenin's tomb a queue was already forming for the opening in five hours' time. From a distance, St Basil's Cathedral looked fairylike, but as we approached we could see that in some places the roof was patched with tin plates, roughly painted, whilst in others the bare wood showed through. Crazy wooden catwalks wandered here and there between the domes. We followed the Kremlin boundary down a steep slope to the bridge over the Moskva River. Palace roofs and church towers, crowned with red stars, clustered behind the wall.

The British Embassy, on the far bank of the river, was formerly the home of a Tsarist sugar magnate. The dignity of the entrance hall, all 'Gothic' mahogany panelling and dark mouldings, was marred by a jumble of Bags stacked ready for removal by the King's messenger. As we waited in the hall a tall figure followed by a very large dog came down the stairs—the Ambassador, Sir Stafford Cripps. A friend in the Embassy advanced us some of the roubles which would result from the clandestine sale of the old clothes we had brought with us. These would supplement our Intourist coupons, which could only be used in hotels or on the Trans-Siberian Express.

After lunch at the Metropole we packed. Our tickets and sleeper reservations were handed out by a dark young man with Jewish features.

'I am your Intourist guide and will accompany you to Vladivostok,' he introduced himself. 'Now we must check your luggage.'

Seeing the pile, and thinking probably of the norm, he looked apprehensive. However, we and the smaller pieces were stuffed into an old car, the rest following, we hoped, in a van.

The platforms of the Kursk Station, open to the sky, were crowded with passengers, many of them for the Urals and points east. Our luggage was now stacked on the platform. Scenting a kill, an NKVD man who had been observing us was joined by another as the Trans-Siberian Express drew in. 'We'll teach them to travel with so much luggage,' he said loudly. Our porters stood immobilized.

'Show me which is yours and I'll help you onto the train with it,' whispered our Intourist 'guide.' 'Be quick.'

Ours was an old Tsarist Wagon-Lits coach, solidly built at a time when ladies and gentlemen travelled with cumbersome baggage. Besides a luggage rack, there was ample storage space extending over the corridor for the length of our compartment.

Kenneth stowed our suitcases rapidly, leaving only a few small objects to be seen in the compartment. 'I'll just go out and help Nick,' he said.

In a moment he was back. 'It's no good,' he said. 'The second

NKVD man saw us taking in the luggage and it must all come out again, he says. Nick seems to be doing all right, but our Intourist chap is in a panic.'

'I'll think of something,' I said urgently. Kenneth hurried out onto the platform.

Something had to be done quickly. Argument would get us nowhere. We had been warned against trying to bribe an official, but a three-pronged attack might be worth trying. Taking a ten-rouble note out of my bag I dropped it on the floor. Close to it I put a bottle of vodka. Then ringing out a hand towel in the small basin next door, I laid it over my eyes and flung myself down on the bunk, feeling nearly as ill as I hoped I looked. The minutes dragged by. Just as I was wondering how long I should have to keep up this act, the door of the compartment opened. My heart missed a beat, but I kept my eyes closed.

'What's going on here?' It was Kenneth's voice, and he was laughing uncontrollably. 'You're not really ill, are you?'

'Almost. Where are the NKVD men?'

'I think they've forgotten us. They're dragging some unfortunate chap off the train. A "speculator", somebody said.'

'Lock the carriage door and let's relax,' I begged.

The compartment, which was to be our home for the next ten days, was comfortably upholstered in crimson velvet with overstuffed arm-rests and plump small bolsters, now a little rubbed and dusty. The dimensions of the carriage were calculated to accommodate sweeping skirts, top hats, swords and uniform greatcoats, as well as ladies' hats piled with tulle and flowers and the entire wings of birds. All the fittings were of solid brass, bursting here and there into leaf and flower. The water in the shower, we discovered, actually ran, though it was cold. After the Metropole, this was luxury.

CHAPTER 22

As the train left the station dusk fell. For the next hour we unpacked and arranged our possessions. The roll of 'Government Property' hung on its loop of string from a brass hook near the window. The books which had survived the customs at Bigosovsk, our patience cards and travelling clocks were fitted into a net attached to the wall.

When soap and toothbrushes were all in place, with our dressing gowns on the back of the door, we felt really at home, and went on a round of visits. Nick, as might be expected, was beautifully organized. Co and Barbara were happily installed next-door-but-one down the corridor, but Dorothy was frantic. She had been assured that she would be sharing with another woman, but her fellow-passenger had failed to turn up.

'The attendant has just been in with a Japanese and I believe they mean to move him in here,' she moaned. 'They're so prudish in Russia and yet they put men and women in the same sleeper. They say he's a diplomat, but how does that help? I shall stand up in the corridor all night.'

'Let's go and talk to the attendant,' I suggested. The attendant, an anxious little man, confirmed our fears. He and his side-kick, he told us, took eight hours on duty and eight hours off the whole way to Vladivostok and back, sharing a shake-down in the cupboard next to the public samovar which stood on a shelf at the end of the corridor. In these circumstances it must have seemed to them most unreasonable that anyone should object to a comfortable bed, especially when the sleeping companion was a diplomat—and Dorothy no longer young.

Dinner would not be served until ten. Meanwhile we must find a solution. In due course the Japanese gentleman arrived with his suitcase and, bowing and hissing, settled into a corner seat in Dorothy's carriage. There was more bowing and hissing as we introduced ourselves and exchanged visiting cards. Mr Shimada, it seemed, had been Second Secretary at the Japanese Embassy in Moscow and was on his way back to Tokyo. There had been no first-class sleeper available, so he had been given a second-class sleeper in the next coach. He could lie down full length at night, he told us, but the upper berth didn't fold back during the day, so that he and his partner found the carriage a little cramped. Now that Dorothy's travelling companion had failed to turn up, he had paid the first-class supplement and was moving in to her compartment.

All this took time to explain, as our only means of communication were Russian, limited on both sides, and German, which Shimada spoke with difficulty.

We explained Dorothy's reluctance to share a compartment with a member of the opposite sex, but it was an awkward point to plug as Mr Shimada was convinced of the innocence of his intentions and of his own faultless behaviour. We begged him to be chivalrous and sleep in his second-class carriage, offering him the freedom of our own during the day.

Our progress was difficult to check, as each time we thought we had convinced him he would bow and smile and say, 'Ja, ja . . . but I stay here.' It was only later that we learnt that in

Japan 'no' is considered a crude word, and is not used in polite conversation.

By dinner time we had got nowhere.

'Come and have a drink,' we said to Dorothy. 'We're making a vodka and celery juice cocktail. Everything will be all right, you'll see.' But our assurances sounded hollow, even to ourselves.

The dining car was arranged with a double row of tables each seating three a side. Two women with cotton handkerchiefs over their heads, and closely resembling the muscular bronzes of the Moscow Metro, were serving bowls of cabbage soup to the diners. This was followed by greyish bread and some rather hard sausage. There was no menu card nor any choice of dishes. Even if the food was not actually harmful, as our American friends had suggested, it was unappetizing and we thought wistfully of the delicious journey provisions we had been obliged to leave behind.

In the few hours since we had left Moscow considerable use had been made of the dining car—or the tablecloths had not been changed since the previous trip, as they were stained with soup and smears of stew left by former diners. So we turned the hanging edges of the cloth back to make use of the clean underside. As the material was coarse, the greasy stains had not seeped through. Unfortunately, at the next meal we found that everyone had copied our attempt at gracious living, so the improvement was only temporary.

This first evening no alcohol was available in the dining car, in spite of Co's attempts at negotiation, only sticky fruit juice. To drink the water on the train was obviously unwise, so we decided to wait for tea from the samovar which was now bubbling merrily at the end of our corridor.

During dinner Mr Shimada sat disconsolately at the far end of the dining car surrounded by some rather uncouth characters—railway workers, probably, with passes to some point along the line. Kenneth walked down and offered him a cigarette. 'We are so sorry that there is no room at our table. Perhaps we shall see you in our compartment tomorrow.' Mr Shimada's reaction was concealed by a deep bow.

'If we can't fix anything by midnight,' Kenneth told Dorothy, 'I'll move into your berth and you can share with Peg.'

When we returned from dinner the attendant unlocked our door. This locking-up was routine when my father was in Russia in 1904, but in those days thieves were an acknowledged hazard. When we asked the attendant the reason for this precaution he just shrugged. He had lowered the upper bunk and made up the beds. A small lamp in its curly brass holder shone down on each pillow.

'You must put your watches on an hour and come to breakfast at nine,' the attendant told us.

Mr Shimada was standing in the corridor. He seemed a little forlorn. 'We were looking forward to sharing our compartment with you during the day,' I ventured. 'It is a pity.'

'Ja, ja,' he murmured, 'but . . .'

I thought of a last desperate move. 'If we are to be separated,' I appealed, 'my husband will be deprived . . .'

'I will spend the morning in your carriage,' Shimada said suddenly. He called to the attendant. 'Take my luggage back.'

He turned to us. 'Till ten o'clock tomorrow.' He bowed and followed the attendant down the corridor.

'What a really delightful chap,' said Kenneth. We told Dorothy the good news. At the moment all three of us felt extremely pro-Japanese.

As we undressed a depressing thought struck me. 'If Mr Shimada comes in at ten and lunch is at three, that makes five hours. And five hours for ten days make fifty. How *can* we talk to him for fifty hours when it is so difficult to keep up a conversation for five minutes, even when we have something urgent to say?'

Next morning we were dressed and ready when the attendant came at nine to tidy away our beds.

'During the night we crossed the Volga,' he announced. This news was also passed on to us by our Intourist man, who seemed relieved to have some positive information to give us about the Journey.

The view from the windows of the train, dimmed by a thick film of grime, was discouraging. On all sides the prairie stretched away featureless and dun-coloured.

When we reached the restaurant car the tables were not cleared and the atmosphere frowsty. One of the waitresses was still stretched out on the floor. (Her normal sleeping place, we learnt afterwards.)

'Seychas' they both murmured and we went back to our carnage.

'They keep Moscow time on the Trans-Siberian,' said Kenneth.

'What! For the whole six and a half thousand miles of it? Does that mean that breakfast and lunch and dinner will get earlier and earlier until we are breakfasting in the middle of the night and having our last meal at lunch-time?'

'No silly, it's only the station clocks which correspond to the time in Moscow, and maybe the time tables too.'

In fact, our meals were produced according to a rhythm devised by the train staff, and this was not always predictable.

We returned to the restaurant car at ten. Though the dirty crockery had been removed the tablecloths were unchanged except that the sides, by now as dirty as the tops, had been turned down again. But the coffee was at least hot, and with an Intourist coupon we were able to get some butter.

Shimada, looking dapper, bowed and pointed to his watch saying with a giggle, 'I am coming *seychas.*'

Ten minutes later he was sitting between us and waiting for the conversation to begin.

We waited too, our three minds groping for something to say. Mr Shimada clearly had a very strong sense of etiquette and we were not sure whether he would approve of the personal questions about family, job and so on, which are such a useful standby.

'In the night we crossed the Volga,' he said at last. This non-event was serving a useful purpose. There was a welcome break when the train stopped abruptly in the middle of an empty stretch of prairie and many of the passengers jumped down onto the track. After only eighteen hours of travel one was suffering from a sense of claustrophobia, and the fresh air and huge emptiness of earth and sky were a relief. Like our fellow passengers we strolled happily in the autumn sunshine.

Suddenly, without a sign of warning, the train started. There was a wild stampede to get on board. The lowest step was two feet above the ground and the handrail out of my reach. A burly Russian threw me up to his friend who reached out and pulled me on board. The rest of the passengers scrambled on somehow and the train gathered speed. Apparently this was a well-known engine driver's prank and accepted as such.

'Never go far away from the train unless the engine driver gets out too,' advised my rescuer kindly.

Shimada appeared to enjoy the joke as much as anyone. Lunchtime was not far off and all three of us were beginning to relax. Kenneth got out the vodka and poured three drinks. Mr Shimada averted his eyes as I drank mine. It was not until three days later that we were sufficiently intimate for him to explain that his wife would not touch spirits. 'It is very *ge . . .*

ish,' he said, drawing out the single syllable in apologetic disapproval.

Lunch consisted of cabbage soup once more and an anonymous piece of stringy meat.

'Isn't there any caviar?' we asked. Caviar, in Russia, was not then regarded as a great luxury, though an awareness was growing that foreigners considered it as something special.

'Tomorrow,' said the waitress reassuringly.

The tablecloths had now acquired a uniform gluey texture due partly to the varying standards of culture of previous diners and partly to the inevitable slopping of greasy soup as the waitresses struggled to maintain their balance against the rocking of the train, so spoons and forks, and even fingers, stuck to the cloth in an unpleasant way.

'Government Property!' we exclaimed. 'We can arrange the sheets to make little clean islands.' When we did this, the waitresses collected them up carefully as soon as we had finished, smoothed them out, and slipped them into their pockets. Evidently they were considered valuable.

'We are not allowed to give tips, but they seem to appreciate toilet paper. Let's ask the girls if they would like some more,' Co suggested.

Both waitresses nodded emphatically. 'But what would you use it for?' asked Co.

'To write letters, of course,' they replied.

'Better cut off the printed words GOVERNMENT PROPERTY,' advised Co. We couldn't risk the girls or their families being picked up as members of an underground group sending out cryptic messages in English.

During the afternoon the train stopped at a busy station.

'Where are we?' we asked our Intourist man. 'What is this place called?'

He was clearly at a loss and jumped down on to the platform to avoid further questioning.

'It must be his maiden voyage,' I said. 'We'll look in the Times Atlas. It's a bit ancient but the maps are beautifully clear.'

From the map it was evident that this must be Perm, the last town before crossing the Urals into Siberia. We hastened to share our discovery with our guide.

'Perm?' he said, puzzled.

'It is Molotov,' said a grim voice. The old Tsarist name was clearly unpopular.

That night we made a few small domestic improvements, stretching a piece of string across our carriage to dry our smalls and puffing a little insecticide into the cracks, just in case.

We were two nights out from Moscow, and European Russia lay behind us. Already we had settled into a comfortably domestic routine as members of a small community. On a really long train journey all impatience vanishes. There is no thought of arrival. No counting the hours. Each day has its own events or particular highlights. One adopts a cruise mentality, content with small amusements, passive while the management takes over control of the journey.

As the train rolled down the foothills of the Urals we sat over breakfast, waiting till Mr Shimada had finished his.

'Murray's Guide says the recommended route from Moscow to Omsk, in summertime, was through Nizhni Novgorod,' I said, 'and then by steamer down the Volga to Kazan and then north up the Kama to Perm. After that one hired or bought a *telega* or *larantass* and horses. It took six days, so you see there has been progress.'

Before the train drew up in Sverdlovsk the Intourist man was knocking at the door of our compartment. He obviously wanted to avoid another awkward confrontation with the Times Atlas.

'We are coming to Sverdlovsk,' he said.

'Have you been a courier on the Trans-Siberian Railway before?' I asked. He shook his head. 'Have you ever before worked for Intourist?' He shrugged.

Dorothy had joined us. 'What do you really do?' she asked.

'I am a student at Moscow University.'

'And what do you study?'

'Well, . . .'

'Are you doing a holiday job?'

His face brightened. 'Yes. You see, my wife has had twins . . .'

It seemed unlikely that a sought-after Intourist job would have been given to an ordinary student who happened to be hard-up.

'And when you get to Vladivostok will you bring a party back?'

'No. I am just looking after you.'

This, and his ignorance of the route and of anything to do with rail travel seemed to settle it. Either he was a trainee member of the NKVD or else he had been co-opted to help deal with an unscheduled group of tiresome travellers.

'I think we should christen him Untourist,' said Kenneth.

We decided to take his story at face value and see if he could do anything to improve our amenities.

'The windows of our carriage are very dirty and we can't enjoy the view. Please can you ask the attendant to see the outsides are done?'

But at Sverdlovsk there was no attempt to clean the windows. Passengers crowded in and out of the train. Queues formed on the platform to buy the few available copies of the local newspaper, though it seemed hardly worth the effort when the contents of the paper were so predictable. Russia was not at war. Her ally, Germany, had for the moment run out of countries to conquer. America was taking a passive, detached role. The only relief to be expected from routine Communist Party propaganda would be the news of a German invasion of England, but with England so small and far away this was unlikely to be of great interest to the inhabitants of a Siberian town.

Sverdlovsk, the former Ekaterinburg, with its factories and foundries and industrial gloom, seemed from the train as unattractive as its history. Memories of the tragic end of the Tsar Nicholas and his family in a cellar only a few kilometres away added a macabre note to the drab actuality of the present town.

The train rolled on through country of a sameness which made any small diversion welcome.

'I read somewhere that at the Paris Exhibition of 1900 they showed luxury coaches built for the Trans-Siberian—a Louis XIV dining car with a ceiling wreathed in flowers and a smoking room decorated with Turkish motifs, and so on,' I told Kenneth. 'To make things more lifelike, a roll of scenery was wound past the windows of the dining car.'

'Unless the scenery is going to become a bit more varied, it can't have added much to the interest,' said Kenneth wearily. 'Just silver birches and prairie with a conifer here and there.'

But there were small alleviations to the monotony. For example, two goods trains, each obviously determined to make use of the same set of points, had collided head on, the locomotives rearing up and plunging down an embankment. The scene had an air of quiet finality. The results of the crash were clear, but how it came about, and why it appeared to have been ignored, was a mystery.

Further on, a stand of silver birches, their trunks all splintered off at half-height, so that they stood up like broken matchsticks, provided another puzzle.

Towards dusk our train stopped at a small lonely station. The air was chill. No one got out. Beside us, on the west-bound line, stood a slow train, the engine puffing black smoke from its great spark-arrester pot. Its bell was ringing. All at once a woman ran across the empty platform. Our train was just moving as she scurried between the coaches. There was a cry, and a sickening jolt as the train came to an abrupt halt. The engine driver came running down the platform and was joined by the guard. They pulled the body out from under the train and laid it, covered with a blanket, on a stretcher. Our attendant was talking excitedly to his colleague.

'The train has cut off her leg. The woman you saw,' he told me. 'She was trying to catch the local to Sverdlovsk and she must have tripped and fallen just as our train started to move. They are putting her in the guard's van and taking her to Novosibirsk.

'But that's nearly a day's journey, isn't it?' The man shrugged. Next morning we asked about the woman.

'She's turning black. I think she's going to die,' he replied, not unkindly.

One of our minor puzzles was that we could never distinguish between the two sleeping car attendants, who looked and spoke alike. To increase our confusion the two shared a copy of Pushkin which they read, turn and turn about, perched on the jump seat beside the samovar.

It seemed to be a point of etiquette on the train not to address a person by name, though we did discover that one of the waitresses was called Galina. This reserve was not due to unfriendliness, we felt, but rather to caution. We were travelling in a cocoon, isolated from the outside world, and however relaxed the passengers might become the journey must end, and there was always an underlying feeling of apprehension.

The landscape had changed overnight and the soil was now the rich dark *Chernoziom*, the famous Black Earth of Siberia. In the official guide to the railway issued in 1900 under the patronage of Tsar Nicholas II, Autocrat of All the Russias, as the title page stated, this was described as the greatest treasure of Siberia, an apparently inexhaustible source of wheat more valued, at that time, than the mineral wealth of the region. Inspired perhaps by the lovely morning the engine driver stopped the train in the middle of a grove of silver birches, their leaves sparkling like a shower of gold coins. Reassuringly he climbed down from his cab.

One of the passengers, described to us as a biologist from Lithuania, did a performing flea act on the rails, balancing nimbly and then hopping from one to another and challenging the onlookers to compete. A tall Soviet officer wearing shiny top boots, ran quickly along a single rail with arms outstretched. Then the engine driver strolled up. Standing on the near side of one rail he swung his arms, flexed his knees and, with a flying jump, cleared the far rail. Smilingly he acknowledged the gasps of admiration and sauntered back to his engine. 'Of course, he's had lots of practice,' muttered his competitors.

Even in Tsarist days, the engine driver took an important part in the social life of the train, mingling with the passengers at stops, shaking hands all round and joining in the conversation. At the best of times engine driving must be a lonely job, even with a colleague to take alternate shifts, but when it goes on for ten days at a stretch some light relief must be absolutely necessary, and a meeting with one's friendly engine driver is reassuring for the passengers.

We had passed through Omsk in darkness and were crossing the Barabinskaya Steppe, a marshy region where the Swiss surgeon Hans de Fries nearly lost his life in the 17th century. 'We remained stuck in the swamps,' he wrote, 'through whole nights, not knowing whether we would freeze to death from the terrible frosts or drown in the swelling floods.'

Things were not much better for the men who struggled for over two years to build the line between Omsk and Novosibirsk across the treacherous ground. Tormented by mosquitoes and engulfed by the swamps in summer, suffering from frostbite and the exhaustion of quarrying in the frozen ground in winter, hauling thousands of tons of ballast to form a firm base for the permanent way, they suffered and died in numbers which could not be accurately recorded.

The line was following the Trakt, the great highway which is still the main land route through Siberia. Along it, over the years, stumbled convicts, chained and branded, sad political exiles, and peasants hoping for land and a new life. The carriage trade of the Trakt, officers, officials, traders and adventurers of all kinds, travelled in horse-drawn vehicles of varying degrees of discomfort.

Our mornings were now occupied with Mr Shimada, and before-dinner drinks in one of the compartments of our group had become routine, but between these fixed events we chatted to fellow passengers wherever the opportunity offered. The Lithuanian biologist was the most informative of our contacts and clearly knew a great deal about Siberia and its history. He was travelling to Chita, where the line to Dairen through Manchukuo splits off from the longer route to Vladivostok.

'I have been sent,' he said, 'on a special assignment.'

'The plague?' we asked.

He shrugged and said nothing.

After lunch our map showed that we were nearing Novonikolaevsk.

'Novosibirsk now,' said the biologist with a twinkle.

A wide river came into view, the Ob, which runs for three thousand miles into the Arctic. It was crossed by nine double spans of a great iron bridge. To the north the river flowed in wide curves bordered with white sand. Houseboats painted in faded turquoise, green and yellow, were tied to the bank. Down the middle of the stream a river boat chugged, awaited by a long queue at the landing stage.

As we crossed the bridge, great blocks of buildings rose to meet us on the opposite side.

'The Chicago of Siberia,' said the biologist.

Novosibirsk was clearly on the up and up. Separated from our platform by broken fences and piles of scaffolding, an immense new station was in course of construction, the wide central arch supported on monumental pillars, the façade pale green and white against a cloudy sky. The current business of the Trans-Siberian was being conducted on a platform of beaten earth splotched with puddles. Unlike previous stations, where queues formed following a rumour that there might be something to buy, here there were stalls selling little felt bonnets and painted toys. A teddy bear, or more probably a replica of a real bear from the nearby forest, dressed in crimson trousers and leather boots, was held up for sale by an old woman. Beside her, a girl with a tray of bootlaces found eager customers. An immense strawstack turned out to be a mountain of last winter's ice, heavily insulated. Men were quarrying the face and loading the ice blocks into the top of a refrigerating car.

In spite of reminders, our carriage windows were as dirty as ever.

'Let's make some wads of damp newspaper and take the ladder for the upper bunk out onto the platform and clean them ourselves,' I suggested.

It was quickly done and the little plush-covered ladder back in place. As we were admiring the sudden clarity of the view, Untourist knocked at the door. 'There has been a complaint,' he said.

'Why? We asked again and again for someone to clean the windows and nothing happened.'

'It is *nyekulturni* for foreigners to do such things,' he replied.

In fact, Untourist was hardly likely to have bothered about the level of culture shown by our behaviour. He might have been nettled at the implied criticism of his efficiency, but his real worry, we decided, was the greatly improved view we had gained of the installations along the line.

At this moment, a stone glanced off the window pane. We couldn't see who had thrown it. Someone as uncultured as ourselves, it seemed.

The line was now running through a gloomy forest, the primeval *Taigá,* which covers thousands of square miles in Central Siberia, forming an almost impassable barrier between the rivers. The men who built the line, the biologist told us, had to struggle with soil which, in the deep shadow, remained frozen until midsummer and then turned, briefly, into a swamp which swallowed up the tree trunks laid side by side to provide access roads for rails and sleepers. Trees, whose roots lost their grip as the surface water drained away, crashed suddenly to the ground. Unfortunately, their wood was too brittle to serve for construction, and timber for sleepers, poles and buildings had to be brought from the Kurgan forests three or four hundred miles away. But to avoid the danger of fire from the sparks produced by the locomotives, the useless timber had to be cleared in a swathe two hundred and fifty feet wide.

In this part of the world the temperature drops in winter to −50°F, whilst at Krasnoyarsk, a little further along the line, temperatures of –67°F have been recorded. We were fortunate to be travelling in early September, avoiding the heat of the Siberian summer as well as the winter cold.

Another pair of trains, buckled and intertwined, were lying at the side of the track. Apparently, the accident rate for goods trains on the Trans-Siberian has always been high, owing to overloading and careless handling, and the harsh conditions endured by engine drivers and brakemen. Passenger trains had a better record, the biologist assured us.

The *Taigá*, with its history of misery and frustration, had already depressed our spirits, and the day was to end horribly. In the inconsequential way to which we were becoming accustomed, we pulled up opposite a siding. A cattle train was standing there, its unglazed windows heavily barred and revealing wooden shelves running the length of each waggon. On the shelves lay creatures so gaunt and unkempt that unless they wore beards it was hard to tell whether they were men or women. Hands like claws, and arms and legs with the skin stretched tight across the bones were thrust through the bars, either in an effort to change an intolerably cramped position or to bring a little fresh air to aching limbs. The spectacle was so horrific that it was hard to believe that it was real. It was a measure of the lack of organization for tourists at that time that our train was carelessly allowed to draw up beside these tragic victims.

'They must be criminals or dangerous subversives, at least,' I thought.

Untourist had come up and was standing beside us, obviously embarrassed.

'What have they done?' we asked.

'Nothing,' he replied in a low voice. 'Just gone for a walk.'

'Pogulat' or 'go for a walk' was the accepted euphemism for changing jobs without having a signature in one's labour book

to show than an employer had given permission. It was only one of many grounds for condemnation to a labour camp.

We had known of the chaos caused by the savage regulations introduced into Latvia after the Soviet annexation: how the workers, embittered by the loss of their social rights and the mismanagement of the Communist political appointees in the factories, goaded by an intolerable piecework system, forced into unpunctuality and abseenteeism by food shortages and the need to forage for their families, and unimpressed by Communist Party incentives, had taken to a go-slow which was entirely foreign to their natures. Thousands of men from the Baltic States had been carried off to labour camps in Siberia, but we had not thought to see a living example of their sufferings.

That night, as we lay wakeful, haunted by the sight of the unfortunate prisoners, the train raced at speed along the track, swaying and creaking and hooting frequently. We hoped that the driver was keeping a close eye on the signals.

Our route from Riga to Vladivostok, via the Trans-Siberian Railway

When we woke next morning the dark Taigá had vanished. The rich black earth was cultivated in a sporadic way, and in the villages the hay stacks were larger than the biggest houses. Patches of vegetables and the cold blue-green leaves of cabbages filled the hollows. On bare grassy slopes cattle were pastured. Behind them rose the dun-coloured mountains of Mongolia.

To our regret, the identity problem of the two attendants had been temporarily solved. The man on duty, his face swollen with toothache, crouched by the samovar. Pushkin lay unheeded on the floor beside him. There was no doubt now which of the attendants was which.

'Isn't there anyone on the train who can help you?' we asked. He shook his head.

'Here are some aspirins. Take two now and two in three hours' time. You must get help in Krasnoyarsk.'

The biologist had joined our morning conversation group and Mr Shimada was asking why the line did not go through Tomsk, once the most important city in Siberia.

'They say the city fathers refused to pay the bribe demanded by the surveyors,' said the biologist, 'so they punished them by taking the line sixty miles south of the town.

'This kept the track straight, saving over fifty kilometres of railway line, so the authorities in St Petersburg accepted it as an economy measure. But it was evident that such an important town could not be left isolated and finally a branch line was built. This required the labour of twenty-nine thousand men and the total cost was far higher than that of a direct line through Tomsk.'

The treatment of Tomsk was only one example of a trend, and many stations were sited at a distance from the towns they served. Of course this suited the local carriers, but was so inconvenient for everyone else that it really seems as though bribery—or rather the lack of it—was involved. The Siberian towns are now growing at such a rate that in many cases they must have flowed out to meet the once distant stations, but one can hardly credit the surveyors with so much foresight.

The town of Krasnoyarsk was coming into view, dominated by what looked like a detached steeple, but was in fact a chapel built by a 19th century gold miner on a spur of rock above the river. The line ran through a confusion of wooden sheds and stacks of timber leading to a large repair depot, the graveyard of hundreds of locomotives in every stage of decay, some slowly rusting away, others stripped to their bare ribs. Rims and spokes of discarded wheels lay scattered on the ground. The town itself had a dreary air.

'Krasnoyarsk is one of the most blissful regions on the entire earth,' de Fries had written two hundred years earlier. 'No place in the world can be found, I believe, where food is so abundant or so cheap as it is here.' However, the inhabitants, he observed, had greatly dishonoured benevolent nature by their revelry, idleness and debauchery.

We walked disconsolately up and down beside the train much as one trudges round the deck on a grey day at sea, hating every minute but doggedly resolved on exercise. At the far end of the platform stood a large wooden notice board covered with photographs, dog-eared and faded by sun and rain. Without exception, the expressions of both men and women were gloomy and even ferocious.

'It must be a Wanted List,' said Barbara. 'But a funny place to put it. Perhaps they hope to stop the villains escaping by train.'

'Those are Stakhanovite workers,' Dorothy corrected her. 'They have special privileges for working harder than anybody else.'

'It doesn't look as though they enjoyed it very much,' Barbara said.

Instead of the usual coat of aluminium paint the standard railway station statues of Lenin and Stalin had been treated to electric blue, and the railway sheds were plastered with Communist slogans.

'Either the inhabitants of Krasnoyarsk are unusually enthusiastic supporters of the Party or the authorities are having a bit of bother with the idleness de Fries talked about,' suggested Nick.

The face of our unfortunate attendant had swollen until one eye was scarcely visible.

'We must find someone to help him,' we told Untourist. Very unwillingly he wandered away into the station, returning with a nurse carrying a small black bag. She made the attendant open his mouth, ran a heavy hand round the swollen jaw and hurried away. That was the last we saw of her. At our request for aspirins she had just shaken her head.

'We've enough to keep him going until we reach Irkutsk,' Dorothy said. 'Let's hope they do something there.'

'Have you been able to sleep?' we asked the poor fellow. He shook his head. But after two sleepless nights he still carried on with his work uncomplaining.

Men with Mongolian faces and fur-lined hats with naps upturned were climbing onto the train. 'Irkutsk, Khabarovsk, Vladivostok,' bellowed the tannoy, and the train moved off to cross the broad Yenisei on a twin eight-span bridge forty feet high, reinforced upstream to withstand the battering of the ice floes in spring.

'The bridges are an amazing feet of engineering,' said the biologist, who had joined us as we looked out of the window. 'Most of the stone work was done by Italians who must have suffered torments in the Siberian winter. The cost of the bridges was alarmingly high—not just in money but in human lives. Men stiffened with cold as they worked on the high spans and crashed down onto the ice below.' He lowered his voice. 'The official story was one life for every million roubles spent, but losses must have been very much higher. The contractors went on drawing the wages of the men who died and no one will ever know the truth.'

'The wicked capitalist system?' I enquired.

'It is human nature that is wicked,' said the biologist quietly.

'Everything was sacrificed to speed, and to save time the engineers went on ahead building the line.'

'But how did the passengers get across in the meantime?'

'In summer they were carried over on ferries attached to a cable which was fixed from bank to bank. A train was waiting on the opposite side. When the rivers froze, rails were laid over the ice. To lessen the weight, passengers used sledges and the train crossed very slowly. Between seasons the service had to be suspended, sometimes for weeks until the ice floes cleared, or the winter freeze-up was sufficient. The bridges caught up with the line remarkably quickly, considering the difficulties and the danger involved.'

We looked back across the swiftly flowing Yenisei to the town of Krasnoyarsk. Against the limitless background of Siberia the squalid spread of the town, which would have been more evident against the narrower skies of White Russia, became insignificant.

The train was climbing slowly through small-forest country with scattered pines and groves of stunted birches, their golden leaves beginning to fall. Here and there a bush, turned crimson, smeared the gold and silver of the birches with a streak of blood. Next morning we woke to drizzling rain and were happy to settle in for a morning with Mr Shimada. He was now busy teaching us as much Japanese as he thought we could assimilate before arriving in his country—and this was very little.

However, we were getting an idea of the immensely hierarchical approach of the Japanese to their language. His pencil flickered over the pages of my sketchbook making complicated designs to show that a wife must use a more respectful form of address to her husband than he to her, whereas both, in their appropriate degree, used less polite forms when talking to a servant. Child-parent conversations were conducted in yet another way. If there had been the slightest hope of our learning enough words to make use of these complicated instructions we might have been worried. As it was, we listened charmed, and wondered what he must have made of manners in Moscow, his first foreign post. The Shimada family fortune was founded on a brewery, it seemed, and he assured us that they also made excellent whisky.

'How sad that your wife can't enjoy it,' I commented slyly.

The rain had stopped, leaving a dreary landscape made even drearier by the mud. We halted at a coal-mining town with gaunt winding gear surrounded by slag heaps. Rolling stock appeared to be in short supply, as a train of box cars was being used to transport coal, which was held in by boards placed across the window openings. I thought of the sessions with Our Friend and wondered if these mines had been the subject of a self-criticism feature lately, and how far they were behind with their targets.

We were approaching Irkutsk, a distance of three thousand five hundred miles from Moscow. Fifty years earlier, passengers using the fastest post horses available had taken thirty-five days for the trip, averaging four miles an hour against our thirty miles per hour.

The train drew into the station and people were jumping off before it stopped, rushing to form the usual queue for a newspaper. Another gallery of grim Stakhanovite faces stared down at us. Just behind the engine sheds stood a parachute tower, looking like something left behind by a travelling circus. In this case, the amusement provided had a strictly practical purpose.

The station platform was heaped with mud over which the passengers slithered, but across the river, between massive new buildings, one could glimpse clustered domes and painted spIres.

During the *belle époque* Irkutsk was christened the Paris of Siberia, but it would have been more apt to call it the 'Manaus'.

Though the two cities were on opposite sides of the world, one isolated in the frozen wastes of Siberia and the other in the steaming rain forests of the Amazon, their origins and way of life were very similar. Irkutsk grew out of the gold rush and Manaus was founded on the rubber boom. The big spenders of both cities built themselves fabulous mansions, sent their laundry to Paris and wore Parisian clothes and jewellery. Manaus built an opera house which was visited by international stars, whilst the inhabitants of Irkutsk paid for a splendid theatre and two permanent companies to play there all the year round. Racketeering was common in both cities, though the streets of Manaus were far less dangerous than those of Irkutsk, which were infested with bandits and garotters. Whilst the streets of Irkutsk were unpaved and ankle-deep in mud or dust when they were not covered with ice, the pavements in Manaus were patterned in black and white mosaic and there was a brisk tramway service and a band of women street cleaners under the competent direction of a Scotsman.

But while Manaus, when the rubber boom collapsed, faded into a ghost town which has only recently come back to life,

Irkutsk, invigorated by the new railway, grew even more important.

Besides being essential for the development of Siberia the railway was urgently needed for strategic reasons. By the end of the century it was clear that Japan was a serious rival to Russian expansionist plans in the Far East and might even menace Russian domination of her conquered territories there. Men and supplies for the Far East had all to be sent by ship from the Black Sea through the Suez Canal and the Indian Ocean, taking a minimum of forty-two days, so a more rapid link was essential for defence purposes. But however many thousands of miles of the Trans-Siberian were completed, the line would not serve for the rapid transportation of troops and supplies until it was viable throughout its entire length.

By 1896 only forty-two miles separated the railhead at Irkutsk from Lake Baikal, whose further shore had already been reached by the eastern section of the railway. The Angara, the only river flowing out of the lake, takes a swift northward course, dividing the city of Irkutsk on the east bank from the railway station on the west. The terrain on the east side of the river offered an easier route for the railway but the surveyors considered that the cost of building a bridge to take the railway over to Irkutsk, and another to bring it back to Port Baikal at the point where the Angara leaves the lake, would be excessive. A survey of the west bank was carried out, unfortunately at a time when the terrain was blanketed under an exceptionally heavy snowfall, and no account was taken of the depth of the ravines to be crossed or the swiftness of the current, which gouged at the river bank. (From the windows of the train we had seen how the scour of the water had cut away the shore so that the wooden houses built near the edge were falling, one after another, into the water. The current at Irkutsk was so rapid that men fishing from barges moored in the river could use it to keep their spinner revolving on the surface.)

For four years the railway gangs toiled, building over fifty bridges, blasting the permanent way out of rock in some places, and making miles of retaining wall in others. By 1900 they reached Port Baikal.

It had always been recognized that the southern end of Baikal, with its clifls falling sheer into immensely deep water, would present formidable problems to the engineers. A hundred and sixty-two miles of track were needed to link the two points reached by the eastern and western sections of the railway. In view of the daunting expense involved the authorities decided to bridge the gap by using ferries.

A magnificent ice-breaker, the BAIKAL, which would carry trains from Port Baikal to Mysovsk, a distance of only about forty miles, was ordered from a shipbuilder in Newcastle. It would provide luxury accommodation for a hundred and fifty first and second class passengers, and deck space for six hundred others. The vessel was taken in pieces to a small ship-yard at Listvyanka opposite Port Baikal, where it was assembled and launched in 1899. Another lighter vessel, the ANGARA, was built and sent over in the same way, but as soon as the ice thickened to a winter depth of five feet she was unable to make any headway unless the larger BAIKAL went ahead to open a passage. Even in summer navigation was not easy. At times great fog banks formed over the lake. At others, storms whipped the water into huge waves.

The authorities decided that the Circum-Baikal loop must somehow be built, and in 1901 work was started. Thirty-three tunnels had to be blasted through the cliffs, sometimes for long distances, and a couple of hundred bridges built to carry the line over torrents and ravines. Unfortunately for the Russians, the

Japanese, in February 1904, fearing that the completion of the Circum-Baikal loop would not long be delayed, attacked the Russian Fleet without warning, and the Russo-Japanese war began.

My father, who was in Russia shortly after this, had told me how Prince Khilkov, realizing that urgently-needed supplies for the army would pile up at the bottleneck at Port Baikal, laid rails across the ice. The temperature was −40°F and tests had shown that the ice cover was thick enough to support rail traffic. But Baikal is treacherous: warm springs produce weak spots here and there and through one of these the first locomotive plunged. After this, rolling stock, lightened of all non-essential parts, was towed across the ice by ropes. The officers crossed in commandeered sledges and the men on foot, a march which even to Tankhoi, the nearest point on the opposite bank, could take as much as thirteen or fourteen hours. The great rifts in the ice, possibly caused by submarine currents, which occur without warning, were a further hazard. One of these buckled great sections ofline, tearing the rails loose from the sleepers. To spread the load, thirty-foot lengths of timber were laid at right-angles beneath the track.

When our train reached Port Baikal the mountains rose almost vertically before us. Two great iron ships, like cumbrous obsolete toys, were moored near the shore. The mouth of the first tunnel, guarded like all the others by a sentry, opened to swallow us up.

Sometimes, between tunnels, one caught a glimpse of the lake, vast and empty. This formidable body of water fills a cleft in the earth's surface over five thousand feet deep by the latest soundings, and stretches for three hundred and ninety-five miles in a north-easterly action. The bed, which is subject to volcanic tremors, is believed to be the source of subterranean rivers and the depths harbour strange prehistoric snails, shrimps and molluscs, and small viviparous fish which disintegrate if they are cast ashore by a storm. Seals have at some remote period found their way into the lake and acclimatized at its northern end.

Where the line crossed a cleft in the mountainside pine trees perched on rocky pinnacles appeared high above us out of the mist, as if rooted in air. Beside a control cabin the railwaymen, or the military, had set up parallel bars and rings to relieve their boredom and isolation, and the stiffness of muscles from hours of sentry-go.

As we entered one of the long tunnels the speed of the train dropped almost to walking pace and great lumps of rock began to fall on the roof of our carriage, whilst water splashed down the windows.

'Surely if we went a little faster not so many rocks would fall on us,' said Dorothy.

'But if there's a rock-fall we should hit it a lot harder if we were going fast,' said Nick consolingly.

The lights of Mysovsk were twinkling in the distance before we gathered for our evening drink, assured now by a steady supply of vodka from the dining car organized by Co. He had also scrounged a tin of apricots, so we strained off the juice and laced it with spirit. Although we could get boiling water from the samovar at any time of day or night, ice was unobtainable, and there is something almost repellent about tepid vodka taken neat. Mixed with any liquid which is not positively unpalatable, it becomes warmly therapeutic.

The moon was like a large slice of water melon when we climbed down onto the platform for a stroll. The dread Circum-Baikal loop, which had haunted the engineers and caused the deaths of so many men, was behind us, and we felt buoyant with relief.

Next morning there was a hint of ice in the clear autumn

sunshine and wisps of mist round the hill-tops. The attendant was perched on his seat reading Pushkin. 'Your colleague. . . ?' we enquired. He beamed and opened the door of their cubby-hole. We were greeted by a symmetrical face and a radiant smile. The abscess had burst. Now we should once more be unable to tell the two apart.

'Only the English helped me,' he said, and wrung our hands. In the restaurant car the tables were spread with fresh cloths, but although it was ten o'clock there was no sign of coffee, or any other passengers.

'You may stay,' said Galina pleasantly.

For days I had carried round a couple of pretty handkerchiefs in the hope of finding the girls alone.

'Put this in your pocket, Galina. Here is one for your friend, too.' She looked round hastily and stuffed the handkerchiefs into the opening of her blouse.

The train was running down a wide valley by a flashing river. The wooden houses had flowering plants in their windows and sunflowers leaned their heavy heads over the small wooden fences. Haystacks resembling large domed beehives clustered in the fields and fat white geese like bundles of clean laundry stretched their naked necks and hissed at the train.

'The biologist has challenged the army officer to a cockfight on the rails,' said Nick at breakfast. 'The train will stop somewhere around midday.' But in fact it stopped sooner, with a great deal of fuss and flurry. The brakes had gone wrong and we were about to cross the Yablonovy Mountains.

'Nichevo,' said the engine driver cheerfully, and the whole train turned out to enjoy the sunshine and the contest, we and Shimada happy to break off our Japanese lesson.

Both the challengers perched on the same rail with their hands locked round their knees, then edged towards each other in a series of small frog-like jumps. The object was to dislodge one's opponent from the rail by barging him, though it was no use being violent as one would then be in danger of falling off oneself. The two men were fairly evenly matched, the officer having the advantage of bulk, though the biologist was very nimble, and he won two bouts out of three. After this, other people had a go, but very few were able even to move along the rail without falling off.

'He is a very famous man,' said the officer, glancing at the biologist. The automatic reticence which we had acquired prevented us from asking why.

The construction of the Trans-Baikal section of the railway had been dogged by labour troubles. Most contractors refused to contemplate the job. Those who did, faced by a categorical refusal on the part of the local Buryat tribesmen to work on the railway, were obliged to employ gangs of convicts, who gained a year's remission of sentence for eight months work. Even so, they engaged in a paralysing go-slow until the contractors devised a piecework system with bonuses for the amount of work done. Output then really looked up, but there were the usual percentage of *varnaki,* or escapees, who made their way back to Russia, thieving and murdering as they struggled through the forests. Peasants living in isolated houses would put out food at night to avoid being attacked by these desperate men or having their houses set on fire.

The terrain, like that between Irkutsk and Baikal, was extremely difficult, and engineers were forced to follow the swift and tortuous course of the rivers, blasting a hold for the permanent way or shoring it up with embankments. In one place the harassed engineers decided to divert the course of a river and lay the line along its bed. As the Circum-Baikal loop was the last part of the railway to be built all supplies had to take the long sea route and be carried up the Amur and the Shilka rivers on barges.

The Yablonovy Mountains gave way to an open plain. In the distance beside a lake lay the town of Chita, low-built and unattractive. It was here that the gently-nurtured wives of the Decembrists, who accompanied their husbands into exile after the failed revolution of 1825, lived out the wretched years.

The station of Chitá is described in the Great Siberian Guide of 1901 as second-class and two kilometres from the town. Forty years later it was still second-class and the town did not appear to have grown much. Passengers for Manchukuo were leaving our train. Normally we should have taken this route to Dairen, saving two days on the journey to the Pacific. Now, only because of the epidemic of plague, we had been allowed to go the long way round to the closed city of Vladivostok. The biologist, to whom we had earlier said a discreet goodbye, was welcomed by a group of officials.

In the Russian section of our Intelligence Requirements handbook the naval base of Vladivostok was designated as a prime target. It was the only Russian naval harbour in the Far East, and the headquarters of their Pacific Fleet. Ever since the Revolution the area had been banned to foreign visitors and we had been unable to obtain any information about the port installations and the naval units based there.

'The plague may have served some useful purpose after all,' said Kenneth thoughtfully. 'Somehow we must get a sight of the naval harbour.'

Breakfast was late and it seemed that lunch was going to be late too. Passengers for the Vladivostok line were not allowed to leave the train, so we moved, as a group, into an empty carriage with wooden bench seats. This proved to have been a mistake, as the carriage was soon invaded by a fiercely unkempt woman with a bucket of water and a scrubbing brush. As the brush swished between our feet Kenneth lifted his so that the woman could clean more easily. With a furious gesture and a torrent of angry words she threatened him with her bucket, calling her colleagues to join in the attack.

'She says the time has passed when you can lift your foot to a Soviet citizen,' said Co, who was trying in vain to soothe her. At this moment, Untourist made one of his rare appearances and the group of women withdrew muttering and leaving a pool of dirty suds on the floor.

That evening over drinks we were seized for the first time with a feeling of boredom.

'By this evening we shall have been a week in the train,' said Dorothy.

'I'm beginning to feel that I've walked every step of the way,' Nick grumbled.

'I did something like that,' said Co quietly.

We all looked up, startled.

'You see, when the Revolution started I was on holiday in the Crimea with a group of school friends and a tutor. Fighting began south of Moscow, so he decided we'd better go across country on foot, hoping to join the White Russians on the way. Somehow we missed them and after more than a year we reached Vladivostok. When we got there we didn't know what to do next. In the end the Red Cross put us in their camp on Russian Island at the mouth of the harbour and I stayed there for over two years, until they were able to trace my parents.'

'Weren't they delighted to see you?'

'They were surprised,' said Co.

I reached for the copy of de Fries. 'Mr de Fries, who did a lot of foot-slogging, reckoned that he took 1,500 steps to a *verst,* that is 2,250 steps to a mile. The distance from Moscow to Vladivostok is 6,524 miles, and from the Crimea just about the same, so that allowing for losing your way from time to time, you'd have taken . . .'

Nick was scribbling on his bridge pad. 'Just about fifteen million steps,' he announced.

Next morning the landscape had only a few birches and pine trees to offer, with stumps to add variety. We went to breakfast at ten by our watches only to find it was officially eleven o'clock and the tables were occupied by passengers hungrily wolfing bowls of stew. Somehow we had got out of step. Mr Shimada hissed rather less politely than usual and, back in our compartment, even encouraged me to drink some of the vodka he had brought from the dining car. The Soviet officer was out of sorts and wandered into our carriage in search of codeine. We were getting quite a reputation as home doctors.

All along the Trans-Siberian Railway Russian influence prevailed. Station staff and most of the people concerned with the line were of Russian origin, but ever since Irkutsk we had seen slit-eyed Mongolians coming in from the surrounding country. Many of these were Buryats who, owing to a religious taboo on washing their bodies, were so filthy that they were shunned by the Russian recruiting officers for fear of contagion. Now, they are adapting to modern conditions and are considered to be the most intelligent of the natives of Siberia.

Looking out of the window after lunch we saw that about a kilometre of the left-hand side of the track was screened by a ten-foot fence made of solid baulks of timber. Just as we were wondering what this blank wall could be hiding, we noticed Untourist standing in the corner and watching us.

The next day we woke up with tummy pains and sampled some of our own remedies. It is strange how much less faith one has in one's own medicine. There is nothing but the label to reassure you, and you miss the obvious goodwill and comforting patter of a human being concerned to help.

At Bureya, needing a little healthy exercise, we started to clean the windows once more. There was no sign of Untourist. Bureya was classified in the Great Siberian Guide as a fourth-class station, but it was charming with its wooden platforms and beds of cherry pie, begonias, zinnias and phlox. Two centuries ago, before invasion and conquest by the Russians and the wholesale slaughter of the Buryat inhabitants, the Amur valley was a fertile area producing abundant crops of wheat. Like Latvia it had suffered the crushing effect of a Russian takeover.

We were following the Far Eastern section of the great Trakt highway. Since this was narrow, there used to be an established rule of precedence, rapid horse-drawn traffic having priority. The great caravans of tea coming up from China were expected to draw aside to let fast vehicles pass, but the drivers, overcome by fatigue or an excess of vodka, often allowed their animals to wander along the middle of the road until they themselves were woken by the lash of a whip.

At Obluchya we got out to enjoy the lovely valley with its meandering river and emerald water meadows. Wooded spurs jutted in from the Manchurian border. Behind them, the mountains were blue. A whole train of flat cars stacked with birch logs drew up beside us. They looked clean and fresh in the shining air, warm now and comforting. Our map showed that we were only three hundred miles from the sea.

Normally Untourist tended to avoid us at platforms, probably fearing more awkward questions. This time he walked boldly up. 'I have to tell you that there have been complaints.'

'Complaints?'

'Yes. You were seen spying on the airfield near Novobedayka.'

'But we didn't see any airfield.'

'No, but you looked.'

So that was it. The great fence. This was farcical, but it could be dangerous.

'We couldn't help looking out of the window. There was nowhere else to look.'

Finding conversation with us profitless as usual, Untourist walked away. But it was an uncomfortable moment. Had someone really denounced us, or was he just trying to demonstrate his zeal? Would the matter be followed up?

We were reading quietly when the train drew in at a station. There was the sound of shots, engine whistles and sirens hooting. We jumped up and looked out of the window. The station name was written up in Hebrew. Sentries with fixed bayonets were posted at the exits. Further down the line a man rushed across the track. There were more shots.

Untourist, as was his habit, had gone to earth, but one of the Russian passengers, an engineer to whom we had lent our copy of Murray's Guide, was chatting to our attendant.

'What's going on?' we asked.

'Nobody knows.'

'Where are we? Is that placard really in Hebrew?'

'This is Birobidzhan, the Jewish Republic which was founded jointly by America and the Soviet Union after the Revolution. Most of the Jews who live here are Russian, but there are a few from other countries.'

The engineer made to get down onto the platform, but a soldier with a fixed bayonet stopped him. He turned to us. 'We'd best sit quietly in the carriage.' He smiled teasingly. 'I hear you're in enough trouble already.' Then he lowered his voice. 'I'm leaving the train at Khabarovsk. You don't know my name and in any case I feel you will not repeat what I say, so for a moment I will speak my mind. It is difficult for a foreigner to understand Russia. It can be difficult even for a Russian. We have adopted many Western ways, but beneath the surface Russia is Asiatic. Serfdom was abolished in 1861. Slavery was not. And I fear that perhaps it never will be . . .'

We were an hour late arriving in Khabarovsk, due to a long wait while we gave first aid to an engine whose driver appeared to be a friend of our own. Though it was already after midnight we decided to stay awake for the crossing of the Amur. Under a swelling moon the great river spread between its banks like a lake. The bridge, supported by an island in the middle, is three kilometres long—the longest in the USSR.

After Khabarovsk the line leaves the Amur and turns abruptly southwards to follow the Ussuri through the maritime territory to Vladivostok.

CHAPTER 23

When we woke next morning the sun was warm and there were small clouds of mosquitoes in the air. To our right the hills of Manchuria rose through the autumn mist. The four hundred and seventy-five miles of line from Khabarovsk to Vladivostok took six years to build. Labour troubles were even worse than in Trans-Baikalia. Chinese coolies imported to work on the line proved idle and inefficient, and were terrified of the Manchurian tigers, which still roam the area. Hundreds of these were shot or poisoned and their hearts and livers, claws, whiskers, bones and blood were dried and ground into a powder which was sold to the Chinese to promote courage. (Now a limited number of tigers are caught each year and sent to zoos and circuses.)

Large sections of the terrain were marshy and treacherous, and swallowed the track as if in a quicksand. Years after the line was completed there were long stretches where the speed of the train could not safely exceed five or six miles an hour.

In order to defend the frontier from marauding Tungu tribes on the Chinese side, Cossacks were given free transport to the banks of the Ussuri, a grant of land, a stock of horses, cattle and guns, and a capital of twenty roubles. For two years, while they cleared the land, the Cossacks were exempt from all but emergency military service. They were so successful in subduing the Tungus that they frequently took their herds across to the Chinese side of the river to graze them on Tungu ground.

After breakfast we found that the upper bunk had not been folded back. This was the last day, and we should reach Vladivostok by evening. At our request, the attendant bundled up our bed linen and restored outward order, and we settled down for our final morning with Mr Shimada. This time, poising two coloured pencils in the air, he drew us a beautiful map of our route to Tokyo, showing the ports of Najin and Chongjin in Korea where our boat to Japan would call. His delicate outlines traced the coast of Japan, the line from Tsuruga on the west coast to Tokio, the intervening mountains, and Fujiyama marked with its exact height. We still treasure this map.

As we were going down the corridor to the restaurant car the Soviet officer pointed out to us a hill where he and his men had fought a fierce battle with the Japs, wiping out a couple of battalions.

At lunchtime we could see that Galina had been crying. 'The chef discovered the handkerchiefs you gave the girls and denounced them to the Train Supervisor, and he took them away,' Co reported.

The chef, with an eye to a deal, told us that food was extremely scarce in Vladivostok and offered to trade our Intourist coupons for cigarettes and vodka. Finally, he included some cheese, a sausage, a piece of cake and a bar of chocolate. During the afternoon we concentrated on packing. As the journey progressed I had made fifty-odd pages of notes, closely written on leaves torn from a small notebook. These I had kept tucked into a money belt round my waist. If the recent denunciation for spying was a sign of trouble to come, then we must be prepared for a body search.

A handbag is among the first things to be examined and is

a dangerous hiding place, so after taking a careful look at our luggage we decided to unpick an inch or two of stitching in the watered silk lining of a small leather holdall. Being light and easy to carry but awkward in shape, this was always put on top of the baggage and therefore kept in sight.

As soon as the notes were safely concealed I began a steady process of auto-brainwashing. 'Your treasures,' I told myself, 'are all in the yellow suitcase. The things you really care about. Be sure that the yellow suitcase is not lost. Keep an eye on it.' In this way I hoped to disguise my real concern and leave in the atmosphere no extra-sensory leads to the holdall.

A milky streak appeared on our left. The Pacific Ocean. Slowly it spread and glistened. The line was now running along the shore, which was clothed in a thin soupy weed, and tiny waves catching the last of the sunset glow.

It was dark when we reached Vladivostok, but the station clock, faithful to Moscow time, showed twelve noon. We were reluctant to leave the train and apprehensive that the trap might, at the last moment, close on us. But nothing happened. Porters, working in pairs, collected our luggage and wandered off, closely followed by us, to find a conveyance to the hotel. A couple of broken-down taxis finally appeared and we bumped off over streets riddled with potholes and deep in dust. Passing through a small square we saw that instead of flowers in the once ornamental garden there were soldiers rolled up in their greatcoats sleeping on the bare earth.

'The lower the standard of living for the troops the easier for the General Staff,' said Kenneth.

'And think what a help in war-time if the civilian population is accustomed to living rough,' I agreed.

The hotel was as dismal as Our Friend's brother had predicted. Once more there was the long wait before we were shown to our rooms, only this time the floor of the foyer was covered in cracked linoleum and the ceiling bulb was so flyblown as to be almost opaque. The manager, a beetle-browed Georgian, made it plain that we were extremely unwelcome guests.

At last he took us to our room. The two iron beds were covered with grimed army blankets. Another torn blanket was nailed over the window. The walls bore the telltale blood splashes resulting from a prolonged campaign against bed bugs. Worst of all, a drunk sat crouched with his head in the wash basin. At this, the manager was actually disconcerted. Giving the man an expert bum's rush, he threw our luggage down and tried to shut the door on us.

'We won't sleep here,' I said. 'It's dirty and disgusting. There are bugs.' But the manager simply walked away. Tired and disheartened, we puffed the last of our insect powder onto the beds and lay down fully clothed.

We woke at five next morning, tortured by flies. The previous night the maid had promised a bath at nine o'clock, but at 8.45 the stove in the only bathroom was cold.

'There will be no bath,' said the maid when we finally found her. Grudgingly she brought a jug of boiling water, but it smelt unwholesome.

Down in the dining room we were joined by the rest of the party. The light was grey and raindrops carved runnels down the dusty window panes. An ancient waiter, patient and timid, brought omelettes like bricks, and soggy grey bread.

'Can we have some butter?' we asked. The manager, scenting a fight, surged in.

'Butter is first-class food. You can't have first-class food for third-class price.'

'Then we will pay.'

'You can't pay. You have no money.'

The sight of some ten-rouble notes mollified him and two saucers of jam were brought. We said that one was enough, but the manager insisted on two, and charged us accordingly. Butter, he said, would have cost three roubles eighty a portion the size of a penny piece. This, at the official rate, would have been nearly four shillings.

In one corner of the dining room a man was lovingly polishing an aspidistra. Its shining leaves were the only things that looked cared-for in the hotel. In the world of the Victorians where interiors were heavy with dust-catching draperies or, as in Vladivostok, grimed from years of neglect, the lush gleaming leaves had an extraordinary appeal.

The rain was still streaming down the windows. To pass the time, but without much hope of success, we pursued the manager up and down the stairs saying, 'We must have a better room.'

'You have only paid for third class.'

'Then we will pay the difference.'

'You can't.'

The manager knew quite well that, having roubles, we could pay the supplement, but he seemed determined to make us scapegoats for the whole party as the other rooms, though drab, were acceptable. An American engineer who travelled across Siberia at the turn of the century, commented on the extreme unpleasantness ofthe manager of the Metropole at Irkutsk. The further east one goes, he wrote, the more disagreeable the managers become. We were at the end of the line and presumably faced with one of the most awkward specimens.

The upstairs loo was out of order and of the two downstairs, one had no lock and the other no seat. 'This is uncivilized,' we complained.

'It is not,' said the manager.

'Then you can't know what civilization is.'

'I do. I've been to New York.'

Dorothy joined in the argument, producing a bug which she had caught in our room and trapped in a matchbox. I thought for a moment that the manager was going to hit us.

'We'd better go for a walk and let him cool off,' said Nick.

So we went out into the rain, determined to find something of interest in Vladivostok. Lying on the lovely Bay of the Golden Horn, it could have been a pleasant place, but it was built in haste when the Russians annexed the territory in 1861—a mixture of garrison and gold rush town. As far as we could see, there was not a single building of distinction.

The dust of the night before had turned to mud which slurped into the potholes left unrepaired since the fighting of the early twenties. The buildings were unpainted and shabby, and even the street names almost illegible, their enamel chipped and scratched.

Dilapidated trams screeched up and down the hills, people hanging from them like bunches of grapes, and jumping on before stops to fight their way inside. Across their prows Communist Party slogans were pasted, their tattered messages fluttering in the wind. Passenger mortality was evidently high, as the authorities had thought it worth while to warn the captive audiences which queued at every stop. Posters depicted people being crushed between trams, or stepping out from the kerb to be flattened. Some warnings even showed a man jumping off a tram and under a car, though this, in view of the scarcity of passenger vehicles, seemed a lesser hazard.

The shop windows in Vladivostok were still pierced by the bullet holes of twenty years ago. Great cracks in the plate glass were riveted together with rounds of metal cut from the bottom of tins. Except for piles of tinned crab, arranged in pyramids and spirals, none of the stock was post-Revolution. In one window bottles of patchouli and violet perfume, rice powder and ivory-handled toothbrushes were thick with dust. The most exciting window display showed a cardboard family, the mother wearing a feather boa and flowery hat, the children in muslin dresses and sailor suits, all playing croquet with real hoops and mallets. A small crowd stood admiring the window—which afforded one of the few diversions of the town. It was all immensely dispiriting.

At lunch, a thin soup was followed by a particularly odious reminder of the gluey tapioca of our childhood days, but this was bright pink and had a fishy taint.

'Caviar,' said the manager challengingly.

'It isn't,' we replied.

'It is,' he maintained. This was repartee on a nursery level.

'The roe from a Pacific fish,' whispered the waiter.

As we struggled to eat the horrible stuff the manager circled the table muttering, 'First-class food. First-class food, and you have only paid for third-class.' We shuddered to think what third-class food must be like.

Despite our determined efforts we had completely failed to find anything of interest in Vladivostok. But what about our sightseeing vouchers? One gold dollar each for the last fourteen days and all we had so far been offered was the man with the megaphone in the Moscow bus. Here was a new bone of contention to keep the adrenalin flowing.

'We have paid for a sightseeing tour every day. When will it begin?' we asked the manager.

'*Seychas*,' he replied mechanically. This remark we felt was to be taken even less seriously than usual.

'We want to go out in a boat.' (This might afford a vital glimpse of the naval harbour.)

'You can't.'

This automatic refusal was no more discouraging than the usual *'Seychas'*. It just varied the dialogue a little.

During all our conflicts with the management Untourist had failed to show up, wisely deciding to keep his head down. Sooner or later, though, he would have to make himself useful.

The only other guests in the hotel, a family of Jewish refugees on their way to Canada, whose luggage tags showed that they were 'Mr, Mrs, Miss and Master April', told us that the boat to Japan would leave in three days' time. If this were true, and we were to maintain our modest standard of living, we should need more roubles.

'There must be a State pawnshop in Vladivostok,' suggested Barbara. 'Let's collect up everything we can spare and take it along.' So we discarded every possible oddment and even some things we found useful, trusting that we could replace them in Japan. The expedition did not appeal to Nick and Dorothy, so with Co and Barbara we crammed picnic things, a watch which had broken on the journey, dispensable clothing, empty biscuit tins, half-used lipsticks and powder compacts into a bag and set out, directed by an old man we met on the first corner.

The pawnbroker would obviously have liked to slam the door in our faces, but he coveted our treasures, particularly the broken watch. After some sharp bargaining we finished with three hundred roubles for the use of our group. Like us, the pawnbroker had time on his hands and decided to treat us to some Communist propaganda.

In answer to every question he declared, *'U nas luche,'* (Everything's better here.)

'How can you say that?' asked Co. 'The shops are empty. Food is scarce . . .'

'Are your shops in England full?'

'Of course.' (We were unaware of wartime shortages.) 'You can buy anything you like.'

'That proves it then,' said the man triumphantly. 'If your workers were properly paid they would buy up everything and the shops would be empty like ours.'

After supper we went out to send a telegram home. The door of the telegraph office creaked as if it had never been opened. The operator sat by a wooden table, fast asleep, his head on his arms. In spite of Co's assurances, he remained deeply suspicious of the foreign text and we felt convinced that he would tear up our telegram as soon as we had left.

As we opened the hotel door the manager scuttled into his office. 'We want to go out tomorrow—in a boat, and fish,' we told him.

'Then you must give me your passports.'

'But you have them.'

'Not I, the police.'

If he expected instant collapse, he was disappointed. 'Then our Intourist courier must get them back,' we said calmly.

Our misery and very genuine grievances had made us reckless, but we were beginning to realize that we had chosen the right line with the manager. The more aggressive we were, the more amenable he became.

'You can have room No.3,' he said to us grudgingly. 'This was a wonderful relief, as we had dreaded a return to the bug-infested bedroom. Our new room, with its pea green dado and pink muslin curtains, was a blissful contrast. What was more, it smelt of paint.

Next morning the sun shone brilliantly. Today we would begin the great boating contest, and carryon with the sightseeing campaign. Already we were beginning to feel tentatively at home, like children who have survived the first week at a particularly unpleasant boarding school.

At breakfast, the old waiter shuffled in with the daily egg-mix brick. Jam appeared and the usual toll was levied. At the going rate, it was costing us something like thirty-five shillings a pound.

Towards twelve o'clock, just as we were preparing to acknowledge defeat and go out into the dismal streets, Untourist came beaming to say that he was taking us down to the harbour.

'You can't have one. boat,' he said. 'You must have two.'

It was easy to understand the logic of insisting on two saucers of jam, since twice as much could be charged for them, but in this case we had already paid for the coupons which were to cover the outing, so nothing was to be gained from insisting on an extra boat. Perhaps this was merely a face-saving device to show that we had not, in the end, got exactly what we had asked for.

The narrow beach was flanked by a row of wooden huts on stilts. As the old man started to push the first boat into the water, two tall men in police uniform strode into the nearest hut. They emerged two minutes later dressed in identical dark blue bathing trunks and each wore his police cap. The old man stared at them apprehensively.

Our boats were sun-bleached and a little unsteady. In the bows of each was a huge life belt. The old man handed us fishing lines—a thick cord tied onto a stripped branch, with a large piece of cork for a float and some rather smelly herring as bait—one set for each boat.

'Bathing is forbidden,' he said. We pushed our boat out into the waters of the Golden Horn, which stretches for four miles to the narrows leading to the open sea.

In the carefree days before the Russo-Japanese War the supposed impregnability of Vladivostok Harbour had done a great deal to bolster the confidence of the Russian General Staff.

Batteries placed on either side of the narrows were reckoned to be able to destroy even the largest naval vessel afloat, but this belief was never put to the test as the Vladivostok Squadron, imprudently venturing out, was destroyed by the Japanese.'

We rowed around in the sunshine, followed at an unvarying distance of twenty yards by the NKVD men. Tiring of this, we halted and lowered the lines. Suddenly, ours snagged. We rowed in a circle, tugging gently in an attempt to set it free. The hook gave, and came up dragging a bunch of black hair.

'We must have hooked a corpse,' said Kenneth.

This suggested to Co the macabre happening at the Black Sea port of Novorossisk, where a group of Tsarist officers were shot and then, weighted down by a heavy chain round their ankles, dropped into the sea. Owing to the preservative effect of the chemicals released by a nearby factory, the bodies did not decay, but could be seen upright and swaying gently with the movement of the water. We decided to give up fishing. As we tried to edge our boats in the direction of the naval harbour, our guardians called that time was up.

Untourist, feeling that he had fulfilled his obligations, joined us at lunch which, this time, consisted of more 'caviar' and half a tin of crab each. During the meal he asked us to introduce him to Miss April who, unlike her raven-haired parents, was a blonde. This was our opportunity.

'We'll get *her* to ask for the sightseeing tour,' suggested Kenneth, 'and she can insist that we come too.'

After lunch we went into the town once more. Under the warm sun the mud of the day before had once more turned to dust. Soon we became thirsty, but where to get a drink? A grubby little kiosk offered dubious-looking glasses of pink water. We decided to try the station buffet, but a woman barred the entrance snapping, 'No buffet.'

Not far from the station was the Military Officers' Club. This was described in the Great Siberian Guide as the most exclusive in town. Now, it was at least neater and cleaner than its surroundings, confirming the impression we had formed right through our journey that the armed forces, together with Party leaders, approved writers, artists and scientists formed the new Russian elite. Paying a rouble each at the door we went in.

The walks were lined with large amateurish portraits of Lenin, Stalin, Voroshilov and so on, rather like the work of an English pavement artist. Benches surviving from Tsarist times had been patched up with new slats and given a coat of paint. By the band stand, a trampled earthen floor was flanked by a placard which read 'MASS DANCING'. Further on we came to a rifle range, and here the notice warned, 'Bring your own gun'. A large rocking horse and some wooden cocks, arranged to be pushed along a set of rails, provided amusement for children. Behind a small cinema advertising an old propaganda film was a magnificent wooden loo with seating for twelve along a single wooden bench. Fortunately, there were no officers in it.

The club grounds were completely empty. It was in fact still exclusive, as the entrance fee of one rouble probably kept the inhabitants out except on special occasions, though the cartons trodden into the ground round the ice cream kiosk showed that there had been visitors at some time.

As we walked home, we noticed a hill which would afford us an excellent view of the harbour.

'We must get Untourist to take us up there on our sightseeing tour,' said Kenneth. This was our one chance. We decided to ask Co and Barbara to come with us. They had no idea of our purpose, but welcomed the idea of an outing.

After breakfast next day there were signs that Untourist was yielding to the blandishments of Miss April. 'He says he will take us after lunch,' she told us. 'I said that my mother would not allow me to go out with him alone.'

We decided to spend the morning trying to find out when our boat would sail. Untourist professed complete ignorance which, on his past performance, was probably genuine. And why should he worry? The trip to Vladivostok was an unsupervised holiday, and enjoying the company of a beautiful girl was something worth prolonging.

The manager answered our enquiries with a curt 'Nyeznaiu' (I don't know), a fact which obviously depressed him. He clearly wished that we would leave Vladivostok as soon as possible, whether for the outside world or for a Soviet prison being a matter of no great interest, though he might have felt that the latter was more suitable.

At three o'clock an archaic Mercedes Benz with rusty paint, frayed upholstery, patched tyres and a cracked glass screen between what was once the chauffeur's seat and the passenger compartment, drew up at the hotel door. Untourist and Miss April squeezed in with the driver, and we four in the back. This was probably an unusually easy load for the poor old car. After a dusty tour of the non-sights of the town we turned up a steep hill, the engine labouring until the road petered out on the crest.

Followed by Untourist and the girl we jumped out. Anxious to show his proficiency as a guide Untourist pointed out the steeple of the former English church, the railway station and the hospital. A few steps forward would give us a better view of the harbour installations. We signed to Miss April. Gently she slipped her hand into Untourist's and led him away over the grass. The naval harbour was spread below us like a model. A light cruiser lay at anchor in the gulf and a destroyer of the Leningrad class in the inlet beyond the commercial harbour. Three large destroyers were moored at right angles to the shore and two similar vessels were under repair in the dockyard. Three or four MTBs with cutaway bows were tied up near the quay and six submarines occupied a small dock. Turning away to avoid suspicion we memorized the whole layout intently. Suddenly Untourist realized the extent of our view.

'Back into the car,' he urged, pushing us in and slamming the door. Miss April curled up beside him, gently stroking his hand.

We hoped that the outing would cost none of us too dear.

Next morning there was still no news of the boat and no more sights we could pretend to want to see. We suggested to the manager that he should swap our remaining sightseeing coupons for a dish of butter, but although they were worth sixty roubles each at face value he refused to make any kind of deal. In the middle of the morning our passports were given back to us with the heartening news that the boat would sail for Japan at five in the evening. The rest of the morning was spent in packing and after lunch we went to see the Japanese Consul to check our visas. He received us in the billiard room of the Tsarist villa which housed himself and his office, and invited us to a game.

'I have bad news,' he said. 'The boat will not sail. It is a Russian "Sunday" and they refuse to unload the cargo.'

On our return Untourist was taken aback that we were so well informed about the boat. In touristic matters he was always one jump behind, and it didn't look as though a successful career in the NKVD lay before him.

If the boat was not to sail, more roubles would be handy, so we made a last hurried trip to the pawnshop. The man offered a hundred roubles for Dorothy's beaded evening bag and only eighty for mine, remarking that hers was bigger, though mine was more intricately beaded.

When we returned the manager was waiting. 'You must all go up to your rooms,' he said.

'Why?' we asked. 'If the boat is not sailing.'

'Very well, you can all go up to one room.'

So we settled down to an apathetic game of rummy. The hours dragged by. Towards seven o'clock we saw from the window the April family, with their luggage, leaving the hotel. Someone turned the key in the door of our room. Our hearts sank.

At eight o'clock the manager unlocked the door. 'Since you ceased to be guests of the hotel at five o'clock there will be no supper,' he said, almost cheerfully.

'Why can't we leave? When can we go?'

'You will be told,' he replied, and went out banging the door. We shared out the two bars of chocolate and the piece of cake from the train, which we had been saving up for an emergency. Ten o'clock and eleven o'clock passed and at midnight, just as we were beginning to despair, we were called downstairs. Our luggage was piled into a shabby bus waiting outside. Untourist shook us each warmly by the hand. The manager, slamming the door of the bus, turned on his heel.

We jolted over the familiar potholes to the quay. The customs shed was filled with a convoy of refugees, most of whom had been there since five o'clock. Perhaps, mental anguish apart, we had been lucky to spend the past seven hours indoors instead of in this cold, draughty shed with nowhere to sit down.

Stakhanovite customs men were still searching the refugees. Having combed their luggage they were now embarking, behind makeshift sacking screens, on body-searching, dragging out gold coins and small pieces of jewellery from the most private places. Rings were pulled roughly from women's fingers and babies' nappies torn off in search of hidden valuables. In the middle of the shed two rabbis, their ritual curls swaying beneath their flat black hats, were intoning a rhythmic prayer. For these refugees, the results of a lifetime of toil and thrift were being annihilated and the years ahead appeared to offer only pain. Some of these people, drained with exhaustion, seemed numb to the final indignities, their faces blank with a merciful anaesthesia.

The examination dragged on endlessly. Parcels of food spilled out in greasy confusion on the examination counter, staining the contents of someone else's luggage. Each unsightly object was valuable, either for its memories, or as some fragile defence against hunger, cold and degradation.

At last our luggage was spread on the counter. Perhaps because his Russian was so fluent, Co had attracted the attention of a particularly keen customs man. We were fortunate in having a white-haired official who handled our clothes tenderly, but was nervous, and passed every book or photograph to a younger man, obviously his senior.

'What is this?' asked the new man, turning one of our 'Government Property' rolls over and over and peering down the middle. To someone who had never come across anything finer than newspaper in a loo, the smooth sheets seemed meant for higher things, and the message printed on each could be propaganda. Without a pang we handed over the remaining rolls. Soon, we hoped, we should be in Japan and surrounded by the loveliest paper in the world.

Dorothy's birthday book gave us an awkward moment. Why should she have chosen to register the date of birth of so many people? Luckily, the official's attention was distracted by the Breusovskaya's receipt for the confiscated tomatoes. Here at last was something he could read, and a useful precedent for his confiscation of our toilet rolls.

The leather holdall was only superficially examined. Finally our luggage was bundled together and piled onto a lorry. Out on the quay it was chilly, but a great moon, almost symmetrical, rode high in the sky. On the far side of the Golden Horn scattered lights twinkled. The merciful darkness hid the dirt and squalor lying behind us, but arc lights shone mercilessly down on the surrounding misery.

At last a series of rickety buses drew up and all the men were herded in. With a sure instinct the Russians had touched a raw nerve of apprehension. As the men were taken off all the women, including ourselves, felt a pang of terror. Why should they separate us? Were the men going to be shot? Would the women be taken away to a camp?

But the buses came back and the women and children climbed in.

An incredibly bumpy ride between sheds, each guarded by a soldier with a fixed bayonet, took us to the wharf where the men were waiting. At the far end the HARBIN MARU was tied up, looking immense and very clean, though in reality she was only a small coasting steamer.

'We can't go on board,' said Nick. 'They only started unloading at midnight and the captain won't accept any passengers until all the cargo is on shore. It's nearly three o'clock and there is no sign of any end to it all. Would you like to go back to the hotel?'

We were unanimous in our refusal, though by now all of us were shivering.

At half past three the Japanese Consul's car drove up and he got out, followed by Mr Shimada. After a consultation with a ship's officer Shimada crossed over to us. 'At the Consul's request, they say you may accompany us on board,' he said. In the Consul's car, meanwhile, a baby's nappies were being changed.

Once more we were first-class passengers and almost free agents. Our narrow little cabin was clean and bare and seemed to us absolutely idyllic. By four o'clock the last of the refugees had come on board and we hoped that the relief would do something to diminish their misery. The mooring ropes were cast off and the ship slowly churned away from the quay.

'Let's go on deck arid see the last of Vladivostok,' said Kenneth.

Co was leaning over the rail. 'Out there is Russian Island where I lived as a boy,' he said, pointing to a dark outline ahead.

'We've got away. We're free,' we called back, jumping in our joy. A dark figure loomed up beside us. A Russian officer in uniform.

'We haven't reached the harbour boom yet,' whispered Co. 'We're still in Russian waters. He'll be taken of by the pilot boat.'

As the pilot cutter chugged away with the officer our last link with the Soviet Union was broken and we felt indescribably grateful.

JOURNEY'S END

The time we spent in Japan waiting for a passage to Canada was a curious blend of aesthetic delights and apprehension at Japan's obvious preparations for war. Dance halls and luxury shops were already closed, and the amount one could spend on meals—even in the most expensive restaurants—was austerely limited. Arriving in Tsuruga, we had been questioned for an hour on end by naval intelligence officers about the ships and submarines in Vladivostok harbour, but it was easy to stall when we had such a limited number of words in common.

Our burning anxiety was for news of the boys, but although we enquired at the Embassy every day, there was no reply to our telegrams.

On every possible occasion we escaped from Tokyo into the lovely countryside. After the vast monotony of Siberia and the drab disorder of the Soviet cities the intricate foliage, miniature scale and delicate outlines of the Japanese landscape were a delight. In order to assimilate what we could of the real Japan we spent, at Mr Shimada's suggestion, a week-end in the traditional Japanese hotel used to accommodate overflow guests from the Emperor's summer palace at Hayama.

On October 26th we embarked on the HIE MARU, bound for Vancouver. For the whole ten days of the voyage the sea and sky were grey. Our cabin bell was never answered and wireless news bulletins were taken down from the board before we were able to read them. On the last evening the captain cancelled his dinner party and we expected that the ship would be recalled to Yokohama at any moment because war had broken out. There was, in fact, still a year to go before Pearl Harbour.

On Sunday, November 7th we landed in Vancouver and set out by train for the east, breaking the journey for four days' recuperation in Banff. The large hotels were closed, but we found a small place where we could read and sleep. Between whiles we bathed in steaming hot pools on the mountain side while storm clouds swept round the peaks and sleet stung our faces. A friendly taxi man took us to the town garbage dump where brown bears sat licking out the empty fruit tins. 'Keep right inside the car,' he warned. 'They get ugly if you haven't any food to offer them.'

In Ottawa we found the longed-for telegram. My mother, unable to communicate with us had, on her own responsibility, cancelled the journey arrangements and the boys were safe in England.

In Ottawa we were told it would be ten days at least before the EMPRESS OF BRITAIN sailed, but if we caught the next train to Montreal we could travel in the DUCHESS OF RICHMOND which was leaving that night. The DUCHESS had come on hard times and was doubling as a troop ship. Blankets slung down the middle of a single dining room divided the first and second class passengers. Men in uniform were sleeping on the floor of the library and the gym. The deck was close-packed with tanks and guns and, since we were not travelling in convoy, the lifeboats were slung out permanently from the boat decks.

With every porthole blacked out, the congestion below decks seemed even more oppressive. One day Kenneth was attempting to reassure Dorothy and me by explaining, with the help of the salt, mustard and pepper pots, that with our speed of nineteen knots no submarine could torpedo us.

'Even if something unpleasant should happen,' he said, 'we would stay afloat for hours.'

'Not with what we've got on board, sir,' said the steward over his shoulder. 'There's two hundred tons of TNT down below.' Life belts had to be carried everywhere and we were told to sleep dressed in readiness for a sudden alarm. One morning we saw, floating on the grey sea, a single lifeboat.

'She's from the CITY OF BENARES,' said the bo'sun. 'Sunk on the 25th of September and seventy-nine of the ninety kids on board lost.' We blessed my mother's instincts.

On the evening of November 29th, after ten days at sea, we sailed up the cold grey Mersey and anchored in mid-stream. The sun had set, but a glare brighter than day shone through any flaw in the blackout. Liverpool was on fire, and no one was allowed on shore.

Next evening, after one of those halting railway journeys which were to become so familiar, the train finally gave up at Willesden, as the line was blocked owing to a bomb. A valiant taxi, circumnavigating burning buildings and crackling over broken glass, took us to the Cumberland where we were offered a room on the fifth floor with window glass, or one on the first without.

Next morning we reported at head office.

'Oh it's you,' said the duty officer. 'We didn't expect to see you for some time yet.'

No mention was ever made of the telegram ordering us to Helsinki. It was assumed to be just another casualty of war.

APPENDIX

THE FIRST WORLD WAR AND LATVIAN INDEPENDENCE

At the beginning of the First World War in 1914 alignment, as far as the Baltic States were concerned, was quite clear-cut. It was, very roughly, Western Europe and Russia, to which the States belonged, against Germany and the Austro-Hungarian Empire.

The German campaign in the East met with success and by the autumn of 1915 the army had overrun Lithuania and Courland. In November 1916, hoping to gain Polish good-will and useful reserves of manpower and grain, the Germans restored the Kingdom of Poland, formerly part of the Russian Empire.

When revolution broke out in Russia in the spring of 1917, the Imperial Government was replaced by a Provisional Government and in November the Bolsheviks took over. Eight Latvian regiments joined the Red Army. The nationalists, who had tried unsuccessfully to negotiate with each government in turn, formed a Latvian National Council and in January 1918 declared that Courland, South Livonia and Latgale had formed an independent republic. This was given *de facto* recognition by France.

By the end of February, however, the whole of Livonia was under German occupation and the Treaty of Brest-Litovsk between Russian and the victorious Germans recognized a German Protectorate in Courland and a temporary German 'police occupation' of Livonia. The Latvian Nationalist movement went underground. Within a short time German troops were within a hundred miles of Petrograd, the former St Petersburg.

The German occupation, though bringing three years of intense hardship to Lithuania and Courland and one year to Livonia and Estonia, probably saved the Provinces from being submerged in the Soviet Union and made the ultimate achievement of independence possible.

The German High Command favoured a straightforward annexation of the Baltic States, which would be merged into a single province and act as a buffer against Russia. Besides being completely contrary to the aspirations of the three nations concerned, this did not appeal to the Centre and Left parties in the *Reichstag,* who feared the accusation of land-grabbing. So, at the instigation of the German authorities, the Courland *Landestag* invited Kaiser Wilhelm to accept the grand-ducal crown of the Province. A similar invitation was extended by the Baltic barons in Estonia. The Kaiser agreed, but no concrete action was taken.

The Estonians, who had been negotiating with the Russian Provisional Government, declared their independence from Russia immediately after the Bolshevik *coup d'etat* in November 1917. The local barons, however, appealed to Germany for military aid and at the end of February 1918 the German army moved in. Nationalist leaders were arrested and all political activity forbidden.

In Lithuania the Germans, anxious to keep a check on Polish power, encouraged the nationalist movement, which was automatically anti-Polish, and allowed a carefully vetted list of two hundred delegates to establish a *Taryba* or national parliament. At the same time, they proposed the union of Lithuania with the house of Hohenzollern. However, the Lithuanians preferred Duke Wilhelm of Urach, who was an alleged descendant of Mindaugas, an ancient Lithuanian king, as their future ruler.

As soon as the Armistice was signed on November 11th, 1918, the nationalist leaders of all three Baltic countries set about drafting the constitutions for their future republics, and a Provisional Government with Karl Ulmanis as prime minister was proclaimed in Latvia. This was given *de facto* recognition by the British.

However, by the terms of the Armistice the Allies ordered the German troops to remain in Latvia, to drive out the Bolsheviks, and withdraw when their usefulness was at an end, but the men were war-weary and mutinous and began a disorderly retreat taking arms, provisions and even rolling stock with them.

The new German Republican Government now recognized the Baltic territories as German-administered protectorates and sent a trade union leader, August Winnig, to takeover in Latvia. Winnig believed that Germany's defeat would lead to an economic debacle and that large numbers of Germans would in order to survive need a refuge, so he was determined that Germany should not lose its hold over the Baltic States. To Winnig's satisfaction he was given the impressive title of Plenipotentiary of the Reich for the Baltic Lands. Alarmed by the advance of the Russian troops and the pro-Bolshevik sympathies of the industrial proletariat, the Latvian Government turned to Winnig for aid.

The Baltic barons, with the help of some White Russians and right-wing Latvians, formed the *Baltische Landeswehr*, or Baltic Militia, and a volunteer German body, the Iron Division, was created to protect the rear of the retreating troops.

Just before Christmas two British warships steamed into Riga Harbour and Ulmanis, the Latvian Prime Minister, asked that the crews might come ashore to help protect his government. The request was refused. The British were told that the Iron Division and the *Landeswehr*, together then numbering about 700 men, were confronting some 16,000 men of the Red Army. However, they insisted that the Germans must hold Riga and recapture all the evacuated parts of the Baltic States. The withdrawal of German troops was to cease. Winnig replied that the troops were disregarding orders and that the fall of Riga was inevitable.

Instead of helping the German forces, the British armed a Latvian Militia which shortly afterwards mutinied and declared for the Bolsheviks. Beyond a brief march through Riga by a small contingent of men, which brought a reprimand from London, the British refused to leave their ships, but carried out a token bombardment of Riga. It was not long before the Russians held three-quarters of Latvia and had set up a puppet Red Latvian Government in their occupied zone.

The Provisional Government agreed that the *Landeswehr* should be officered by Germans. Latvian citizenship, with the right to settle, was granted to any German who served in the Iron Division for at least four weeks. This brought a rush of volunteers from Germany, many of whom were unaware that they were to engage in fighting.

At the end of November 1918 the Russian Council of People's Commissars declared Estonia a Soviet Republic. The country, weakened by the German occupation and stripped bare by the retreating troops, was in no state to oppose the Bolsheviks and by December 10th the Red Army was advancing westwards from Pskov and down the coast from Petrograd towards Tallinn. A heavy bombardment by British warships drove the Russians back. The British provided arms and supplies and the Estonians also received support from the White Russian Northern Army.

By February 1919 the Red Army was driven out. In the absence of an industrial proletariat, the Russian attempt to turn Lithuania into a Soviet Republic met with little success and, after four months of Soviet domination the capital, Vilnius, was captured by Polish legionaries and the Provisional Government moved to Kaunas.

The Russians were intent on creating a Soviet Republic of Latvia which they hoped to use as a channel for the now of Communist ideas to the West, and as a model for a non-Russian Soviet Republic. Conditions under the Bolsheviks were appalling. The bourgeoisie were stripped of money and possessions and obliged to exchange homes with working-class families. Forced labour was introduced and food rationed in three categories, the lowest being allottd to the sick, the elderly and those not considered socially desirable. Revolutionary tribunals ordered anyone suspected of liberal sympathies to be shot without trial.

The Russian success, coupled with the fear that the Red Army would succeed in making contact with revolutionary groups in Germany, now galvanized the Germans in Latvia into desperate action, and they sent for General Rudiger von der Goltz, who had just completed a successful campaign against the Bolsheviks in Finland, to take command of the Iron Division. Goltz was determined to recover the Baltic States for Germany and quite prepared to disregard any orders from the

Latvian Provisional Government. The British distrusted Goltz and, since he obtained most of his supplies by sea, established a blockade of the coast of Courland.

The governments of the three Baltic States had pleaded with the Allies for *de jure* recognition of their independence, but the status of these countries was less important than the continuation of the struggle against Bolshevism. The Allies were supporting the White Russian Admiral Kolchak, who had set up an all-Russian government, called the Directorate, at Omsk on September 23rd, 1918. Kolchak had no intention of allowing the Russia for which he was fighting to be deprived of its Baltic coast.

To add to the confusion caused by the Allied support of three conflicting forces—the White Russians, the Germans and the nationalist governments—there was disagreement between the British and the American Military Missions. The Americans disapproved of supplying arms to the Latvians, and of the Baltic blockade.

On April 16th a detachment of the *Landeswehr* under Baron Hans von Manteuffel, arrested the Latvian Government, and Ulmanis was obliged to take refuge in a Latvian ship, under British protection. A puppet government was set up under a Pastor Niedra, who had escaped from Russian-occupied Riga disguised as a Red Army officer. German-led forces captured Riga on May 23rd.

The Allies, alarmed at this German success, sent a commission to the Baltic to arrange for the raising and equipping of native Latvian, Lithuanian and Estonian troops. The Latvian Government was to be reinstated and von der Goltz relieved of his command. The German Republican Government disowned Goltz's actions and said that as soon as a truce was concluded between Soviet Russia and Germany their troops would be removed. The Allies, however, offered to allow Goltz to remain, provided that he would organize the recruitment and arming of Latvian troops and help in the establishment of a Latvian coalition government. Goltz, instead, ordered the Iron Division to advance northwards, but was met by Latvian and Estonian forces at Cesis and soundly defeated. The Iron Division and the *Landeswehr* withdrew to Riga.

On June 10th, General Sir Hubert Gough, in charge of an Inter-Allied Mission, ordered Goltz and the Niedra Government to retire to Courland and allow Ulmanis to set up a Latvian Government once more. The *Landeswehr,* under the command of a British officer, became a unit of the Latvian army.

In spite of an order signed by General Foch for the evacuation of all German troops from Latvia by August 30th the commanders delayed, hoping that if they waited till the winter freeze-up British sea power would be hampered and they could procrastinate still further. The German Government dreaded the return of the Iron Division's soldiers who, disappointed of their promised lands and, owing to trade union regulations, unable to obtain employment in Germany, would present a subversive threat.

An ingenious idea occurred to von der Goltz. The remnants of the White Russian Northern Army, led by Prince Anatol Lieven, had decided to join the German volunteer forces in Liepaja as a first step in a plan to cut the Moscow-Petrograd railway. They were joined by other White Russian units under the adventurer Bermondt. If a West Russian Government were formed in Berlin, the German volunteers could be granted Russian citizenship and join Lieven's forces. The Allies would then have no legal basis for insisting on their return to Germany, and the German Government could disclaim all responsibility.

Before this scheme could be put to the test the White Russian General Yudenich, acting on British instructions, ordered Lieven to proceed to Narva on the Estonia-Russian frontier, leaving Bermondt in command of the growing White Russian forces in Courland. Whilst professing devotion to the White Russian cause Bermondt felt that the German side had more to offer. The 30,000 Germans under his command, however, found themselves converted into 'West Russians', a status which they did not take too seriously. They were paid in notes printed by Bermondt, using as security the booty which he hoped to capture.

Bermondt invited the Latvians to co-operate in the capture of Moscow, but they ordered his immediate withdrawal from the country. Against the advice of Lieven he attacked Riga, but was forced by a joint British and French bombardment to retire to Jelgava once more.

The Latvians drove Bermondt's forces into Lithuania, where they were twice defeated and struggled homewards, leaving a trail of looting, murder and rape. On returning to Germany they werre given a hostile reception.

By December 1919 the evacuation of German troops from the Baltic States was complete. In January 1920 the Latvians, with the help of the Poles, were able to drive the Red Army out of Latgale. The frontier between Latvia and Estonia was settled in March, though that with Lithuania was not established until March 1921.

Once treaties had been signed between the Baltic States and Soviet Russia the Allies' last hopes of restoring a non-Communist regime in Russia vanished and they were willing to give *de jure* recognition to the three countries. The independence of Latvia and Estonia was recognized by Britian and France on January 26th, 1921. Owing to the dispute over Memel Lithuanian independence was not acknowledged until December 20th, 1922.

ABOUT THE AUTHOR

Winifred Margaret "Peggie" Pollock Benton was born in 1906 in Malta, where her father was serving as a military doctor and her mother, as a nurse. She married Kenneth Benton, an English teacher, in Vienna in 1938 at the outbreak of World War II. Kenneth was recruited into MI6; their work during the war included contributions to the Bletchley Park decoding project and intelligence gathering for the "Double Cross" plan, which successfully misled the Germans about the location of the D-Day landings.

After the war, Peggie translated and authored cookbooks. She also completed and published books started by family members, including *Peterman* and *One Man Against the Drylands*. Peggie was working on a sequel, *Drylands Bear Fruit*, just before her death.

INTEGRATED MEDIA

Find a full list of our authors and
titles at www.openroadmedia.com

FOLLOW US
@OpenRoadMedia